Thinking about
the Future

Thinking about the Future

George P. Shultz

HOOVER INSTITUTION PRESS
Stanford University | Stanford, California

Hoover Institution Press Publication No. 699
Hoover Institution at Leland Stanford Junior University,
Stanford, California 94305-6003

First printing 2019
25 24 23 22 21 20 19   7 6 5 4 3 2 1

Manufactured in the United States of America

The paper used in this publication meets the minimum Requirements of the American National Standard for Information Sciences—Permanence of Paper for Printed Library Materials, ANSI/NISO Z39.48-1992. ⊗

Cataloging-in-Publication Data is available from the Library of Congress.
ISBN: 978-0-8179-2254-2 (cloth. : alk. paper)
ISBN: 978-0-8179-2256-6 (epub)
ISBN: 978-0-8179-2257-3 (mobi)
ISBN: 978-0-8179-2258-0 (PDF)

Contents

Introduction

This book is about the future. I have always felt that you can learn about the future—or at least relate to it—by studying the past and identifying principles that have continuing application to our lives and our world.

Take the idea of accountability, which inspires my first chapter. The American people love sports because they always involve accountability. If you catch a pass, you gain some yards; if you drop it, you've lost a down. Accountability applies in the marketplace, politics, governance, and throughout daily life. The idea has been on my mind for a long time, and a few years ago I applied it to the problem of terrorism in a lecture in London at the invitation of Lady Margaret Thatcher. Going forward, accountability will take on new dimensions. How should governments think about accountability as digital communications give instant information to citizens everywhere?

Then there's the importance of trust. When you don't trust someone, you have a hard time dealing with them because you don't know if they'll deliver on their part of a deal. When you know they will deliver, you trust them, and then you can deal with them. Trust is the coin of the realm, the foundation of all transactional behavior and in fact all productive human behavior.

The idea of trust is illustrated in my account of my relationships in Israel, contained in chapter 2. As related in that story, there was a dramatic moment when Prime Minister Yitzhak Shamir was to give his decision on an American proposal. Everyone expected a long period of negotiations, but he said simply, "You know our dreams, you know our nightmares. We trust you. Go ahead."

I learned a lot from my relationships with Israelis. This is set out in a relatively new essay, but the US-Israel relationship has been central for many years. I described it at length in 1985 at the Annual Policy Conference of the American Israel Public Affairs Committee.

Some forthcoming questions were not flagged quite so clearly in the past, but there are still enough old principles and practice to guide us into the future. As I describe in chapter 3, big technological changes are afoot in the world, and some of them will create stunning changes in the way we work and where we do that work, as well as in warfare. I mentioned information and communications, and that is joined by emerging revolutions in machine learning, in manufacturing, and in our ability to manipulate biology and our environment. Obviously, we need to analyze these developments with abundant care, so as to understand how to take advantage of what they allow us and how to deal effectively with the problems they pose. I wrote on this topic recently in a *Wall Street Journal* op-ed ("America Can Ride the 21st Century's Waves of Change," June 27, 2018).

But we also need to remember that this is hardly the first time our society has seen major change. Not that long ago, a large proportion of the population worked on farms. With the growth of efficient agricultural practices, only a small number of people are now running America's farms. About six decades ago, I was a young man on the MIT faculty. The buzzword then was *automation*, and everyone thought it implied that huge changes were on the horizon—and they were. But what I wrote then could apply to the world today, *mutatis mutandis*. That means we should understand the new developments and find ways of adjusting to them, mainly through education and training. But we need to have the right balance of taking advantage of the good and dealing with the difficult.

Some quandaries endure. Chapter 4 considers the drug problem, for instance, which simply won't go away. In many respects it seems to be getting worse: more Americans now die from drug overdoses each year than were killed during the hostilities of the Vietnam War. In America, we started working on the issue in the

Nixon administration. The idea was that if you prevent supplies from coming into the country, people will not have access to them. I remember one incident when I was director of the Office of Management and Budget—a story I retell in the chapter. Senator Daniel Patrick Moynihan and I were heading to Camp David, and Pat is exuberant. Pat says, "Don't you realize? We just had the biggest drug bust in history!" "Congratulations," I say. Pat continues: "We confiscated fifty tons of cocaine!" I say, "Great work." Pat: "Don't you realize? We've broken the French Connection." Finally he comes around: "I suppose you think that as long as there is a big and profitable demand for drugs in this country, there will be a supply." I look at him and say, "Moynihan, there's hope for you." The supply-oriented approach has simply not worked, so it is time to try something else. I have been suggesting that change for a long time, and I will keep doing so.

I admired the late great economist Gary Becker, so when I was invited to give a talk at his eightieth birthday, I accepted and took as my topic the war on drugs. I put it all in the context of some of Gary's suggestions on the subject interspersed with my own views. I wrote again on this topic more recently with my friend Pedro Aspe, who saw this same issue from another perspective as secretary of the budget and secretary of the treasury in Mexico.

Well, there is hope, and we can look at examples such as the success of Portugal in dealing with drugs. Portugal maintains the illegality of drugs but decriminalizes their use so that people can go to treatment centers without the threat of being apprehended and incarcerated for their use of illegal drugs. New technologies and business practices will continue to reduce the costs to discover, manufacture, and distribute illicit drugs, just as they have throughout other legal consumer sectors. Governments should look carefully at the creative experiments in dealing with this problem offered by Portugal and other countries or states. Otherwise they will simply repeat the failures of the past.

Another important topic is the use of force. Our future echoes the past as we must once again seriously contemplate our defense capabilities and interests in comparison to peer powers. Chapter 5 gives a framework to think about that problem. In the Reagan period, as brought out in the talk I gave at the Marine Corps University in 2017, we were very careful in the use of force. But we nevertheless developed great strength. Strength is what gives you the results you want. When you use force successfully, it gives you strength, as in our small-scale invasion of Grenada. But when you use force unsuccessfully, as in Afghanistan, that strips you of strength because it shows that you cannot accomplish what you set out to achieve.

At any rate, it is important to understand the interplay between force and strength because if you're ever in a position to make decisions about this issue, it is well to have learned from experience and to know how to use force successfully. But one should appreciate the basic importance of strength.

Force also has an ethical dimension, as I brought out in an address at the convocation of Yeshiva University in New York in 1984. As President Eisenhower said in his 1958 State of the Union address, "Military power serves the cause of peace by holding up a shield behind which the patient, constructive work of peace can go on."

Right now, in the United States and practically throughout the world, we are struggling with problems of governance—the focus of chapter 6. How do we solve the problems and take advantage of the opportunities before us? This issue is of overriding importance, and I have thought about it for many years. In 1970, as secretary of labor, I gave a talk titled "The New Federalism" at the University of Chicago's Graduate School of Business. I argued for greater reliance on states and cities to administer whatever programs were agreed upon. We see similar trends today, given the diversity of interests and capabilities even within our own country. What might a "New, New Federalism" look like as this country takes on a variety of new governance questions in a fast-changing technological environment and with close personal impacts? In a speech titled "Steady as You Go" to the Economic Club of Chicago in 1971, I emphasized the importance of strategy to the success of any plan, be it related to the economy, governance, or other areas. Today, leaders in democratic countries are increasingly distracted by short-term reactions to this or that. Into the future, deliberately setting out a strategy—working from one's own agenda—will only become more important for effective governance.

As our traditional global partners struggle with their own domestic crises of governance, the world is likely to look to a strong United States for guidance. But chapter 7 shows that effective foreign policy doesn't just happen. You need a strategy, and to implement that strategy, you need resources. I explained all this in testimony before the US House Appropriations Committee in 1987, but the argument is just as relevant today; for instance, in the question of how to deal with refugees. Of course migration pressures are likely to grow, as global demographic growth shifts toward areas with lower productivity. Will the movement of peoples across the globe follow the path of mobility in goods and finance from recent decades? I also testified on this issue, explaining how the Reagan administration approached the subject.

Chapter 8 addresses one tricky new sort of governance problem for this generation and those that follow: the changing environment. I have been working on the issues of climate change for a long time, and I set out my concerns with a nod to past experience in a *Washington Post* article, "A Reagan Approach to Climate Change," in March 2015.

For many years, I have advocated for a revenue-neutral carbon tax, for instance in an op-ed I wrote with James Baker, titled "A Conservative Answer to Climate Change," which was published in the *Wall Street Journal* in February 2017. Since that article appeared, the idea has been gaining ground, and many companies have signed on to it, giving it traction. I think these ideas will take on increasing relevance as the scale of the emissions problem becomes more obvious and demonstrates the need for a strategic framework toward this problem that is compatible with our other economic and social interests.

Another issue of overriding importance to the United States and the world is, like climate change, being passed from my generation to those yet to be born, and I conclude with that. This is the proliferation of nuclear weapons. The damage that can be done by any nuclear exchange is incalculable.

Right now, I think the way forward has to be reestablishing the ability to talk sensibly with the Russians about this subject. In the speech I gave at the Marine Corps University, I pointed to the "Pershing moment" (the deployment of nuclear-armed ballistic missiles in Germany despite a great effort by the Soviet Union to block such deployments) as a turning point in the Cold War. It was preceded by a strategy. I discussed that strategy in my testimony, reproduced here, at a US Senate Foreign Relations Committee hearing.

Suppose we have a modern "Pershing moment" with Russia sometime soon and it becomes possible to once again establish a sensible dialogue with them. Is there any hope of reaching an agreement to severely limit the number of nuclear weapons or even eliminate them altogether? There is a slight basis for hope and for a program to follow up if the idea materializes.

In a meeting of the Valdai Discussion Club on October 19, 2017, Russian president Vladimir Putin said the following:

> The world has entered an era of rapid change. Things that were only recently referred to as fantastic or unattainable have become a reality and have become part of our daily lives.
>
> The . . . issue is that ICAN [International Campaign to Abolish Nuclear Weapons] has brought forth a new attempt, or a new path towards bringing about a world with less, with fewer, or with no nuclear weapons. This is one of the few new initiatives on the horizon at a time where many of the established policies are bogged down and are not moving at all. And I do not think anybody should be surprised that the Norwegian Nobel Committee focuses on nuclear weapons. No single issue has been singled out by the Nobel Committee more often than nuclear disarmament. Ten Nobel prizes has [sic] had this in its rationale, so nobody should be surprised.
>
> *Fyodor Lukyanov*: Then I will have to try to convince you, Mr. President. If they have awarded ten Nobel Prizes; and even in our time, our country—then the Soviet Union—put forward the idea of a complete ban, maybe we should return to it?

Vladimir Putin: Our colleague from the Nobel Institute is partly right.

If you ask me whether nuclear disarmament is possible or not, I would say, yes, it is possible. Does Russia want universal nuclear disarmament or not? The answer is also yes—yes, Russia wants that and will work for it. This is the good part.

However, as always, there are issues that make you think. Modern high-tech nuclear powers are developing other types of weapons, with higher precision and only slightly inferior to nuclear weapons in their destructive force. Nuclear weapons include bombs and missiles that hit large areas, carrying a powerful charge that affects a huge territory with the power of both the explosion and radiation. Modern high-tech armed forces are trying to develop and put into service high-precision weapons, which come close to nuclear weapons in their destructive power; not quite, but close.[1]

Not long afterward, in February 2018, the United States produced its latest "Nuclear Posture Review." It begins with this statement:

The United States remains committed to its efforts in support of the ultimate global elimination of nuclear, biological, and chemical weapons. It has reduced the nuclear stockpile by over 85 percent since the height of the Cold War and deployed no new nuclear capabilities for over two decades.

Nevertheless, global threat conditions have worsened markedly since the most recent 2010 NPR [Nuclear Posture Review], including increasingly explicit nuclear threats from potential adversaries. The United States now faces a more diverse and advanced nuclear-threat environment than ever before, with considerable dynamism in potential adversaries' development and deployment programs for nuclear weapons and delivery systems.[2]

These two statements show the difficulties of nuclear disarmament, but at least they give a basis for hope. How do we go about realizing that hope? If we get back to constructive dialogue with the Russians, we should address with them the subject of nuclear disarmament.

Previous efforts have always been confined to the United States and Russia (or the Soviet Union)—understandably, since these two nations hold most of the world's nuclear weapons. But this time, we should reach out to other states with nuclear weapons and invite them to join us in an attempt to rid the world of nuclear weapons. Such an enterprise might later gain support from the recent UN effort by the non–nuclear weapons states for the elimination of nuclear weapons, as noted in Putin's comments. This work should proceed with care and energy.

Henry Kissinger, Senator Sam Nunn, Bill Perry, and I have given a lot of thought to this problem, and we have written several opinion articles on the subject. Two of these pieces, reproduced here, are "A World Free of Nuclear Weapons" (*Wall Street Journal*, January 2007) and "Deterrence in the Age of Nuclear Proliferation" (*Wall Street Journal*, March 2011).

To pull all of this together, I also include a powerful sermon on the subject of nuclear weapons by Bill Swing, former Episcopal bishop of California and current president of the United Religions Initiative. For years I have attended Bill's sermons in San Francisco's Grace Cathedral, just down the hill from my home. Its eloquence underlines the urgency of the problem today.

CHAPTER 1

Accountability

Accountability

Accountability is an idea central to the functioning of our society, our world economy, our security system, and much else about our lives. Of course it applies to problems of ethics and morality, which are so much at issue in the United States today. But accountability also has an operational aspect: individuals and institutions, whether public or private and regardless of ideology, make better choices when they are held accountable for their actions.

This idea has been around a long while. The Gospel According to Luke tells the story of Lazarus and the wealthy man, which demonstrates that everyone eventually faces a reckoning for their actions—if not in this life, then in the next. And accountability has had great resonance in America since its founding. As a boy, George Washington, the story says, took his hatchet and cut down a cherry tree. When questioned about it by his father, George made himself accountable for his act. This is just a story, we are told; it never really happened. It was supposedly concocted to give color and make an inspiring moral point in a popular biography of Washington. But the story keeps on being told. I saw a political cartoon based on it just a short while ago. So it must convey something of significance to ordinary people. In the first instance, of course, it's a story about telling the truth. But deeper than that is what it says about accountability. When you do something, you ought to be accountable for it.

This seems to me to explain the persistence of the story and why, although it is a children's tale, it says so much about America. Our country is founded upon each individual's freedom to think, speak, and choose. That won't work unless each person is accountable for his or her acts of free choice. And the political system of individuals in America is representative democracy. We vote, and when those we vote for win the election, we want them to know that they will be held accountable to the voters for what they do with the mandate they have been given.

The story of our country hinges in a way on issues of accountability. "No taxation without representation" was a demand for accountability from one's government that helped give birth to the United States. The Civil War was fought because the slave states could not be allowed to escape accountability for their practices by departing from the Union and continuing to operate under their own rules. And America's painful decisions to take part in World War I and World War II—which we could have avoided, protected as we were by two great oceans—demonstrated our willingness to be an accountable member of the small community of free nations ready to resist tyranny.

* * *

In my formative experiences as a grammar school student, I had the good fortune of falling under the tutelage of some good, tough teachers who had high standards. I remember one occasion when I was daydreaming, and suddenly an eraser—thrown by the teacher, who was a good marksman—hit me on the side of the head. His message was "pay attention," and he held me accountable to do so. His name was Dux Beaumont. He taught math. Also accountability.

Later in life, I played football, basketball, tennis, and then golf. And among their lessons, perhaps the most penetrating has to do with accountability. In team sports, you have a job to do in your position, and the success of the team depends on everybody doing a good job. You want to be a contributor. You want to be a part of the team. Under those circumstances, you hold yourself accountable, as does everyone else on the team. Those who don't carry their share of the load aren't appreciated. That's how you get sent to the second team. But, to my mind, individual sports like tennis, and especially golf, are games of ultimate responsibility. You are the one who tees up the ball. You hit it. It comes to rest somewhere. Eventually you get it on the green. Maybe your caddy or your partner helps you, but in the end it's up to you to decide on the speed and break in the green and to hit the putt. The ball comes to rest, and either it is in the cup or it isn't. There is nothing ambiguous about the result.

When I went back for my senior year at Princeton, I was in about as good physical condition as I had ever been in my life. I was determined to make the first team in football. As the fall practice unfolded, I was really doing well. This was going to be my year, I thought. Then in one of the scrimmages I was clipped—blocked from behind—across my knees, and my left knee was badly wrenched. I managed to get off the field, but when doctors examined the knee, they determined that was the end of my football career. What a disappointment.

Then an interesting development took place. I was invited to be the coach of the freshmen's backfield. In those days freshmen didn't play on the varsity team. As it happened, the incoming freshmen included a lot of talented players. I had learned quite a lot during my three years at Princeton, so I had the task of trying to help these new, talented players as much as I could. This was my first experience in what is commonly called teaching. But it was an especially instructive one for me because, as I reflect about it, I was hardly in a position to be a normal kind of teacher. What emerged was an exciting environment of learning rather than teaching. I found that the job of trying to get something across to people was a real learning experience for me. And so it shaped a lot of my thinking about not only how to handle myself as the teacher in the classroom but also how to manage. It has always seemed to me if you can create around you an environment where everyone feels they are learning, including yourself, you are going to create a very hot environment. People are going to be excited about what they are doing. You have to insist that they go home at night. That is the one of the ways you can manage people effectively. They sense a sharing of responsibility and accountability, although, as the leader, you must accept the ultimate accountability because the decisions are finally yours.

* * *

The essay that follows develops this idea of accountability in leadership and reality's relentless judgments. Through my years in government, I had long been concerned with the problem of terrorism, stretching back to the 1983 bombings of the US embassy in Lebanon and then six months later our Marine Corps barracks there. I remember the day I awoke around two o'clock in the morning to the news that 241 Marines had been killed in a suicide truck bomb there—it was the worst day of my life. Decades later, the attacks of September 11, 2001, opened a new chapter in that threat for the United States. Shortly after those attacks, I was invited by my friend Margaret Thatcher to make a speech on the US-British relationship, so of course our nascent response to terrorism was at the front of people's minds.

At that time, I chose to frame the problem in terms of accountability. As close allies, the two countries should respond sharply to attacks so that states who made deals with or tolerated terrorists, as well as the terrorists themselves, knew they would be held accountable for their actions. Global changes, like the spread of information, have made the fundamental job of governing a diverse citizenry more difficult. But the state remains an important part of the system of international accountability. At the same time, Osama Bin Laden and other potential terrorists had to understand that they could not escape retribution simply because they

were not sovereign states. And the War on Terror that followed set out to do just that.

With the experience of history in the years since, it's
clear that the results of that campaign have been mixed—
particularly in regard to the aftermath of the Iraq War, the
intelligence for which was wrong and the consequences of
which we were not sufficiently prepared for. You could say
that the United States and her allies today have faced their
own form of accountability for those choices, just as they
have throughout history, and as they will continue to into
the future.

A MORE ACCOUNTABLE WORLD?

Address delivered for the 2001 James Bryce Lecture on the American Commonwealth at the Institute of United States Studies, London, November 5, 2001. Edited for length.

You honor me greatly, Lady Thatcher, by your presence here tonight and by introducing me in your own country. You and Ronald Reagan produced a revolution by the power of your ideas and by your ability to put those ideas into operation. You ended the Cold War, you led the way to the elevation of freedom as an organizing principle in political and economic life, you changed the world and so very much for the better.

In doing so, you also became the symbol of the greatest national partnership in history: Britain and America. Our steadfast relationship once again, at this very moment, is fighting on a far-off frontier for freedom and security—for ourselves and for all decent people.

James Bryce, whom we honor through this lectureship, explained the strength of the Anglo-American bond: how our common heritage, developed in different styles, laid the foundation for democracy, progress, and the rule of law around the world.

Bryce's remarkable work, *The American Commonwealth,* gave Americans a gift we could not have given ourselves. As President William Howard Taft said, "He knew us better than we know ourselves."

As a Californian, I should also note that James Bryce was the first British ambassador to the United States to visit the West Coast. A man whose intellectual energy produced a ceaseless flow of written observations on his travels fell utterly silent during his stay in San Francisco. We have nothing whatsoever on record from him then. The new mansions on Nob Hill built by the rail and gold rush millionaires, the Golden Gate (even before the bridge), the squalid and violent Tenderloin, the flood of immigrant Chinese workers must have presented such an amazing sight that even the great Bryce could find no words for it.

* * *

Recently, I have been working on the question of accountability, the importance of holding people and institutions, public and private, accountable for their actions.

Without accountability, without a sense of consequence, a mentality takes over that says, "I can get away with it." That is true whether you are talking about individual behavior or corporate or national reactions to bailouts, acts of genocide, and much more. Right now the issue is terrorism. So this evening, I want to look at terrorism through the lens of accountability.

The monstrous acts of al-Qaeda have now made the principle of state accountability the law of nations. After the bombings of our embassies in 1998, the Security Council stressed "that every Member State has the duty to refrain from organizing, instigating, assisting or participating in terrorist acts in another State or acquiescing in organized activities within its territory directed towards the commission of such acts" (Res. 1189). On December 29, 2000, the council strongly condemned "the continuing use of the areas of Afghanistan under the control of the Afghan faction known as Taliban . . . for the sheltering and training of terrorists and planning of terrorist acts" (Res. 1333). Then, after September 11, 2001, the council accepted the position pressed by the United States and Great Britain recognizing the inherent right of self-defense, stressing "that those responsible for aiding, supporting or harboring the perpetrators, organizers and sponsors of these acts will be held accountable" and reaffirming that every state is duty bound to refrain from assisting terrorists or acquiescing in their activities (Res. 1368 and 1373).

The legal basis for the principle of state accountability is now clear, and the right of self-defense is acknowledged as an appropriate basis for its enforcement. Our actions now must make that principle a reality.

* * *

Then Prime Minister Margaret Thatcher, after a terrorist attempt on her life in Brighton's Grand Hotel on October 12, 1984, spoke about terrorism with characteristic strength and candor: "The bomb attack on the Grand Hotel early this morning was first and foremost an inhuman, undiscriminating attempt to massacre innocent, unsuspecting men and women. . . . The bomb attack . . . was an attempt to cripple Her Majesty's democratically elected Government. That is the scale of the outrage in which we have all shared; and the fact that we are gathered here now—shocked, but composed and determined—is a sign not only that this attack has failed, but that all attempts to destroy democracy by terrorism will fail."[3]

Speaking two weeks later in reaction to Brighton and other acts of terror, I developed her themes: "We cannot allow ourselves to become the Hamlet of nations, worrying endlessly over whether and how to respond. Fighting terrorism will not be a clean or pleasant contest, but we have no choice. . . . We must reach a consensus in this country that our responses should go beyond passive defense to consider means of active prevention, preemption, and retaliation. Our goal must be to prevent and deter future terrorist acts."[4]

The Heads of the Group of Seven major industrial democracies meeting in Tokyo on May 5, 1986, stated that we "strongly reaffirm our condemnation of international terrorism in all its forms, of its accomplices and of those, including governments, who sponsor or support it. Terrorism has no justification."[5]

This unprecedented international manifesto came about through the toughness and determination of Margaret Thatcher and Ronald Reagan, but the other leaders were fully on board.

These statements from the past show that terrorism is a weapon with a long history, used by states and groups hostile to free societies and operating in ways designed to make it hard to know who has committed an atrocity. They also contain the key ideas necessary for success in the fight against the terrorists and their state sponsors. . . .

* * *

I have listened carefully to the many powerful statements, formal and conversational, made by President Bush since September 11. Here is how I understand his strategy.

The conceptual heart of the president's approach is contained in four big ideas. First is this: we are at war, and we are at war with terrorism. That's a big change from the way our government has looked at this in the past, as a matter for law enforcement: catch each criminal terrorist and bring him before a court. That is not war. A war is fought against an enemy bent on the defeat of your country. The object of war is to use all necessary means to eliminate the enemy's capacity to achieve his goal. So a big, important difference in concept is at work when you go to war.

The second big idea is that our enemies are not just the terrorists but also any state that supports or harbors them. Terrorists don't exist in a vacuum. They can't do the things that they aspire to do unless they have a place where they can train, where they can plan, where they can assemble equipment and their deadly weapons, where they can gather their intelligence and arrange their finances. They have to have a place, they have to be sheltered and helped by a state. So the president has been saying to everybody, "Watch out. We are not only after the terrorists, but also the countries that hide them, or protect them, or encourage them." The president seeks to make any state that harbors terrorists accountable and therefore so uncomfortable that they will want to get rid of them, so in the end the terrorists will have no place to hide.

The third big idea is to get rid of moral confusion—any confusion between the terrorists and the political goals the terrorists claim to seek. Their goals may or may not be legitimate, but legitimate causes can never justify terrorism. Terrorists' means discredit their ends. Terrorism is an attack on the idea and the practice of democracy. Terrorism for any cause is the enemy of freedom. So let us have no moral confusion in this war on terrorism. As long as terrorism exists, civilization is in jeopardy. Terrorism must be suppressed and ultimately eliminated.

President Bush's fourth big idea parallels what Ronald Reagan, as a presidential candidate, said in an address on August 18, 1980, written out in his own hand:

> We must take a stand against terrorism in the world and combat
> it with firmness, for it is a most cowardly and savage violation

of peace. . . . There is something else. We must remember our heritage, who we are and what we are, and how this nation, this island of freedom, came into being. And we must make it unmistakably plain to all the world that we have no intention of compromising our principles, our beliefs, or our freedom. That we have the will and the determination to do as a young president said in his inaugural address twenty years ago, 'Bear any burden, pay any price.' Our reward will be world peace; there is no other way to have it.

War. No place to hide. Moral clarity. Freedom. There are all sorts of words that go with this grand strategy: *determined, realistic, patient, tough*—and don't forget *smart*. Americans are smart and so are our principal partners, the British. We have to work at this not just with our massive capabilities but with those great national characteristics by which our peoples traditionally are known. *Yankee ingenuity* is an old phrase. And the British, as the names of Royal Navy warships tell us, are *Indefatigable, Intrepid*, and *Indomitable*. We do unexpected things. And we never give in.

The American people get it. All of a sudden, the American people understand that here is this phenomenon that is dangerous to us—to our way of life—and we are going after it. No doubt success will take time. No doubt there will be bumps and potholes along the road. But we will be determined. And we will remember who we are and we will live our lives as they should be lived. As Margaret Thatcher put it in 1984, we are "shocked, but composed and determined." . . .

* * *

The president has declared war on terrorists and the states that harbor them. No place to hide. This idea underlines the importance of the sovereign nation-state, an entity with the capacity to govern and therefore to be responsible for what takes place within its borders. That is one reason for the emphasis on helping countries—Afghanistan right now—learn to create for themselves a stable government, remembering their history, developing their own pattern of representation, and giving hope to people that the future can be better than the past. But we must remember that when a state ceases to function, chaos is given license.

But the war to hold terrorists accountable for their evil acts and to hold states accountable for acts of terror that originate within their borders compels us to look closely at the foundation of order and progress in the world.

We live in an international system of states, a system that originated over three hundred years ago. The idea of the state won out over other ideas about how to organize political life because the state gave people a sense of identity, because it provided a framework for individual freedom and economic progress, and because states over time proved able to cooperate with each other for peace and mutual benefit.

The state has made its way in the world by beating back one challenge after another. In the nineteenth century, the idea of nationalism tried to take over the state and turn it into an instrument of aggressive power.

In the twentieth century, Communism in Russia created a monstrous totalitarian tyranny.

The Nazis took power in a state, convinced they could transform it into a "Thousand-Year Reich," an empire based on prestate fantasies of racial purity.

In our time, the state has been challenged by global currents that have eroded its authority. Information, money, and migrants move across borders in ways far beyond the traditional means of state control. Nonstate entities encroach upon state responsibilities from below while international organizations draw sovereign state powers from above.

As states have appeared weaker, terrorists have moved in on them. Many states in response—and in the false hope of buying time or protection—have taken damaging actions that only further diminish their own authority and legitimacy. States in every part of the world have avoided accountability when it comes to terrorism, and now we are paying a heavy price.

Some states have made tacit deals with foreign terrorists, allowing them offices in their cities in return for a pledge of immunity.

Some states have tolerated, subsidized, and facilitated home-grown terrorist groups on the understanding that they will not attempt to overthrow national leaders, creating a kind of grotesque protection racket.

Some states pump out huge volumes of propaganda against other states to direct terrorists within their borders toward external targets.

Some states, in a desperate search for legitimacy, have invited religions that foster terrorists to take over substantial sectors of governmental activity on condition that some functions, such as foreign affairs and defense policy, be left alone.

And some states secretly, but undeniably, support terrorism directly as a matter of state policy.

Every one of these deals between states and terrorists is an abdication of state accountability to its citizens. If these deals are not reversed, the states that make them and ultimately the international system of states will not survive. That is why the war on terrorism is of unsurpassed importance.

For all the realities of globalization that have drained authority from the state, no other basic entity of international life can replace it. The state is all we have as a means of ordering our international existence. Other forms may challenge but none can replace it in its most important function: the state is the indispensable institution for achieving representative government and for protecting individual rights.

If we falter in the war on terrorism, more and more states will make accommodations with terrorism. Ultimately, the consequences for world peace, security, and progress will be catastrophic.

But if we are creative and resolute, more and more leaders and citizens will regard our determination as an opportunity to clean up and liberate their own societies and to reconstitute the principle of accountability in their states.

Right here, in this hall, we sense the heritage of freedom and courage that is ours to uphold. We have the examples of Baroness Thatcher and President Reagan, of the prime minister and president today, and of the great leaders and valiant people of our countries in centuries past.

With this inspiration, we will surely succeed.

CHAPTER 2

Trust

CHAPTER 2

Trust

There is a lot of talk these days regarding the personal relationships among world leaders, their interactions even orchestrated for public effect. I think of the photograph of President Reagan on horseback with Queen Elizabeth at Windsor Castle, or of President George W. Bush driving a pickup around his ranch with Vladimir Putin. President Barack Obama's apparent friendship with South Korean president Lee Myung-bak was credited in part for the creation of the first free trade agreement with an East Asian country. Today, Japanese newspapers report on "golf diplomacy" between Prime Minister Shinzō Abe and President Donald Trump, speculating on the strategic implications of relative handicaps.

In my experience it's hard to say how much of a difference these sorts of personal friendships or chemistry make in international relations. It's always easier to talk of friendship when the other conditions for interaction are good. And too much focus on maintaining "the relationship" can even get in the way of taking on important but potentially divergent interests.

What does matter, though, whether you are on opposite sides of the Cold War or you are two countries in the same neighborhood, is trust. Trust is the condition on which any

Prime Minister Margaret Thatcher meets with President Ronald Reagan, Secretary of State George P. Shultz and other cabinet members in the garden of the Hotel Cipriani on the sidelines of the 13th G7 Summit in Venice, Italy on June 9, 1987.

other positive interaction depends. It is the personal currency that leaders earn and then spend when they do what they say they are going to do. Trust allows for credible interactions with both friends and foes—and it is something that I have depended upon throughout my own career in government.

I recall a time when I was secretary of state under President Ronald Reagan. My Soviet foreign minister counterpart was a man named Eduard Shevardnadze. He was from Georgia, and his wife was from Georgia. We developed a trusting relationship in the sense not that we agreed with each other but that we were candid and clear. At one point, he asked for a private meeting, and he says to me, "George, we have decided [note the past tense] to leave Afghanistan. We haven't decided when, and we haven't decided when to announce it, but we've decided to leave." He said, "I'm telling you this so that maybe you and I can talk a little bit about how to have this happen in such a way that we minimize the loss of life in the process." He could never have told me that if he thought I would go to the press or something. The only person I told was President Reagan. It did wind up that it was possible to work out something; we had a big conference in Geneva and in the end worked out the parameters.

Another time, I recall how President Reagan stood up for something to preserve a trusting relationship, even though it wasn't popular to do so. It was the Cold War, and the president was set to visit Germany. Months earlier, German chancellor Helmut Kohl had been photographed shaking hands with French president François Mitterrand in Verdun to symbolize the new era in relations decades after the Second World War. Kohl asked if President Reagan would be willing to do the same, and the president agreed, Kohl himself having recently weathered political opposition to support American Pershing missile deployment goals in West Germany.

The German side suggested we do the ceremony at a military cemetery in a village called Bitburg, an active American air base near the Luxembourg border. The White House quickly looked things over and accepted the plan. Once announced, though, the press started to look into it in more detail and found that a number of German SS officers had been buried there. The domestic uproar was understandably harsh. Holocaust survivor Elie Wiesel spoke out about it at a White House event, noting that the American president's place was to stand not with the SS but rather with its victims. In the end, President Reagan modified the trip to include a visit to the Bergen-Belsen concentration camp so that his intentions would be clear but went ahead with the Bitburg ceremony as he had promised.

A short while later I was on a trip to London, talking with Margaret Thatcher. Unprovoked, the prime minister observed to me, "Ronald Reagan is probably the only political leader who would take such a beating at home to deliver on a promise. But it tells you that when Ronald Reagan gives you his word, he is good for it."

But I learned the most about the importance of trust from my dealings, over a long time, with Israel. Israel maintains itself by being strong, but it also remains committed to the same shared values we hold as Americans. You work best with Israelis or any other people if you realize that trust is the coin of the realm. As a small state in a tough neighborhood, credibility is a resource not to be squandered. This idea is at the heart of all good human relationships.

Two essays related to my experiences there follow. The first is a major policy speech on Israel I delivered to the American Israel Public Affairs Committee (AIPAC) in 1985, when I was secretary of state. At the time, we were greatly concerned that the country's poor economic conditions would result in instability, with regional security implications. Following that is a recent reflection on my relationship with Israel—its interests and its fears—delivered in San Francisco in 2017 to a gathered conference of Soviet Jews. These were the so-called refuseniks, who were on my mind as I made that first address in the 1980s and who became an important human rights aspect of our dealings with the Soviet Union during the Cold War.

THE UNITED STATES AND ISRAEL: PARTNERS FOR PEACE AND FREEDOM

Address delivered by Secretary of State George P. Shultz before the Annual Policy Conference of the American Israel Public Affairs Committee, Crystal City, Virginia, April 21, 1985. Edited for length.

We Americans are united by values and ideals that have guided us since the founding of this nation. We seek to preserve and promote freedom: freedom to vote, freedom to speak, write, think, and worship as one chooses. We believe in tolerance—and religious tolerance, in particular. We believe in justice and equality under the law. We are committed to democratic governments as the best if not the only way to protect the rights, well-being, and dignity of all men and women.

We have also understood that to pursue these noble goals, we have to be strong enough to defend our country and our way of life against aggression. And we must have an equally strong commitment to international peace and security. A world of peace offers the best hope for the spread of freedom, and a world of freedom offers the best hope for lasting peace.

In the latter half of this century, both the defense of freedom and the achievement of peace have come to depend on American strength. There can only be peace when potential aggressors know that they cannot hope to achieve their aims through war. In the modem world, this means that America, as the strongest democracy on earth, has a responsibility to stand with those who share our hopes and dreams.

These principles inform every action we take in our foreign policy. Today, I would like to talk about how our ideals, our morality, and our responsibilities in the world apply to our relationship with Israel and to our hopes for peace in the Middle East.

The United States supported the creation of the state of Israel almost four decades ago because of moral convictions deeply rooted in the American character. We knew of the centuries of persecution suffered by the Jews, and we had witnessed the horror of the Nazi Holocaust. No decent American could fail to see the justice and necessity of a Jewish state where Jews could live without fear.

But the founding of the state of Israel also had a wider significance. Certainly, America's support for Israel has been a moral response to centuries of persecution. But the birth of Israel also marked the entrance onto the world stage of a new democracy, a new defender of liberty, a new nation committed to human progress and peace. In a world where such nations have always been the exception rather than the rule, the creation of Israel was a historic and blessed event.

When Lincoln spoke at Gettysburg of rededication to the cause of freedom, he was saying that the survival of liberty depended on people's faith in liberty. Israel's success as a thriving democracy helps sustain our faith in the democratic way of life not only in America but throughout the world. Today, the principles of freedom and democracy are more alive than when Israel was founded. The number of countries around the world that are democratic or on the road to democracy is growing. I believe the example of Israel and the United States has something to do with this heartening trend.

No wonder, then, that the friendship between the American people and the people of Israel has grown so strong over the years. Our original moral commitment to Israel has never wavered, but over the years Americans have also come to recognize the enormous importance of Israel—as a partner in the pursuit of freedom and democracy, as a people who share our highest ideals, and as a vital strategic ally in an important part of the world. The moral and personal bonds that tie us together have strengthened us both.

America's Commitment to Israel's Security

For all these reasons, the United States has maintained unwavering support for Israel's security for nearly four decades. Until peace was made with Egypt, Israel had been completely surrounded by hostile forces since its birth, and it has had to fight four wars in less than forty years to defend its very existence. We know that the goals we share with the people of Israel—freedom and peace—cannot be achieved unless both America and Israel are strong. That is why we are committed, and always will be committed, to helping Israel protect itself against any combination of potential aggressors. And that is why we must always make clear to the world—through our material and moral support for Israel, our votes in the United Nations, and our efforts for peace—that we are a permanent, steadfast, and unshakable ally of the state of Israel.

Every year we provide more security assistance to Israel than to any other nation. We consider that aid to be one of the best investments we can make—not only for Israel's security but for ours as well. Even as we developed our own budget and worked with Israel on its economic program, we nonetheless went ahead with a major increase in our security assistance for Israel. This is a statement of our commitment; it reflects our understanding of who our friends are in the world and who can be counted upon in times of crisis. Americans know that we have no more reliable friend in the world than Israel.

Our common interests afford us an opportunity—and impose a necessity—to work together on many issues.

We face, for example, the common threat posed by the Soviet Union. The American people and the people of Israel both know what is at stake in the struggle against the spread of Soviet power: not just territory and natural resources but the very way of life for which both our nations have shed so much blood and made so many sacrifices.

The continuing persecution of Jews and other minorities by the Soviet government is an abomination. And we in America know that a threat to the rights of Jews anywhere is a threat to the rights of all peoples everywhere. In the Soviet Union today, Jews are not free to practice their religion or to teach Hebrew or Yiddish to their children; they are actively discriminated against throughout the government and society.

In the face of this injustice, hundreds of thousands of Jews seek to leave the Soviet Union. Many want to settle in Israel. But Soviet authorities continue to restrict Jewish emigration, and only a tiny number are allowed to leave. Those who have sought emigration and been denied exit visas often suffer additional persecution; those who stand up for their rights risk prison or confinement in so-called psychiatric hospitals. The United States is doing all it can to urge the Soviet Union to set the Jews free. Nothing the Soviets could do would further convince us of their desire to improve relations than to release Anatoly Shcharansky and others and grant Soviet Jews their right to emigrate.

In addition to denying human rights at home, the Soviet Union has also consistently sought to undermine the strategic interests of both Israel and the United States. Today, they seek to increase their influence in every corner of the globe, including within this hemisphere. . . .

The Challenge of Peace

Americans are committed to the security of Israel because we want to ensure that the Jewish nation and the Jewish people never again face a threat to their very existence. But our permanent commitment to Israel's security serves another, related goal as well: the goal of peace.

Military might has prevented defeat on the battlefield, but true security and peace can come only when Israel has gained the acceptance and recognition of its neighbors. That is why, even as we assist Israel's capacity to defend itself, the top priority of our efforts in the Middle East is to promote Arab-Israeli peace through negotiations.

We have learned many important lessons over the years. One of them is that a strong, visible, and permanent American commitment to Israel offers the best hope for peace. The history of the Arab-Israeli conflict shows without question that movement in the peace process can only come when there is no doubt of our commitment to Israel. It can only come when no one in the Arab world or elsewhere has any delusions about the central reality that America's support for Israel can never be weakened. Israel has demonstrated, beyond doubt, that it will not bend or change its policies in the face of military or terrorist threats. Nor will the policies of the United States ever yield to terror or intimidation. On this principle, the United States and Israel stand together, solid as a rock. So others should not miss the point: the point is to be sure people recognize there are no military options. There are no terrorist options. The only path to progress, justice, and peace in the Middle East is that of direct negotiations.

Negotiations work. We have tangible evidence of this today in the peace treaty between Israel and Egypt. This relationship is the cornerstone of the peace process. We must build upon it. The Egyptian-Israeli relationship itself must grow and be strengthened. And others must learn from the example that Egypt and Israel have set. President Mubarak is committed to peace. Others must join him. We are glad that King Hussein has reestablished Jordan's diplomatic relations with Egypt. The process of building peace must continue, and the United States is committed to helping the parties move forward.

In recent months, there has been much activity. Many people on both sides are working to further the peace process. Today, for the first time in years, there are signs of a new realism and a new commitment on the part of key regional actors.

Prime Minister Peres had made clear Israel's desire to negotiate with Jordan without preconditions, and he has expressed his great respect for King Hussein. The king has also called for peace; he has undertaken an effort to organize the Arab side to negotiate peace with Israel on the basis of Security Council Resolution 242. There is also movement in the Palestinian community toward greater realism, and President Mubarak has played a constructive role in promoting negotiations.

Both Arabs and Israelis trust us, and they seek our help. They find reassurance in our participation as they face the risks and challenges of peace. Such an American role is indispensable.

We also know that those Arab nations moving toward peace are taking risks. Radical forces in the region use terrorism and threats of war not only against Americans and Israelis but against responsible Arabs who have worked to bring Egypt back into the

Arab fold and who have sought to promote negotiations with
Israel. As King Hussein took steps to move with the Palestinians to
the negotiating table, we saw Jordanian diplomats killed; we saw
Jordanian airline offices bombed. Those who take risks for peace
should know that the United States will help them defend themselves. The United States must continue to support those who seek
negotiations and peaceful solutions against those who promote
violence and oppose peace. . . .

Assistant Secretary of State [for Near Eastern and South Asian
Affairs] Richard Murphy is now in the region, on the president's
behalf, exploring practical steps that might be taken toward peace.
But whatever opportunities may emerge, no one in the region or
throughout the world can have the slightest doubt about America's
policy: Israel's vital interests will never be compromised; Israel's
survival and security will never be put at risk.

At the same time, we have also made clear our concern for the
Palestinian people. Lasting peace and security for Israel will require
a just settlement for the Palestinians that ensures their dignity and
legitimate rights. How ironic and tragic it is, therefore, that those
who claim to act on behalf of the Palestinians have continued to
block negotiations—the only course that can achieve a just settlement for the Palestinians.

Now is the time for the Arabs to let negotiations proceed. Now
is the time for the Arabs to let King Hussein come forward. There
is no alternative to direct negotiation; the longer this truth is
evaded, the longer the Palestinian people are the victims. Those
who chased illusions of "armed struggle," those who engaged in
terrorism, those who thought that Soviet support would intimi-
date the United States and Israel have only brought death to inno-
cents and prolonged the suffering of the Palestinian people. Such
methods have achieved nothing constructive and never will.

But a way is open for progress—even early progress—and we
know what that way is. President Reagan's initiative of September 1,
1982, remains the most promising route to a solution. Our policy
will continue to be guided by six fundamental principles in the years
to come.

First, we will continue to seek a lasting peace that respects the legitimate concerns of all the parties.

Second, the United States will oppose violent and radical challenges to peace and security. We will oppose governments or terrorist organizations of whatever stripe in their efforts to undermine the state of Israel and our Arab friends in the region.

Third, US policy toward the PLO [Palestine Liberation Organization] is unchanged: we will never recognize or negotiate with any group that espouses violent solutions or refuses to accept Resolutions 242 and 338 or recognize Israel's right to exist.

Fourth, the only way to achieve a genuine, lasting peace is through direct negotiations between the Arab states and Israel. No other procedures can substitute. No other approach will get anywhere. No further plans or preliminaries are needed. There is one and only one place to negotiate: at the table, face to face.

Fifth, we will support a negotiated settlement by which the Palestinian people can achieve their legitimate rights and just requirements. We will not support the establishment of an independent Palestinian state in the West Bank and Gaza, nor will we support annexation or permanent control by Israel.

Sixth, and finally, we will always insist on Israel's right to exist in peace behind secure and recognized borders. As President Reagan said on September 1, 1982—part of his initiative—"In the pre-1967 borders, Israel was barely ten miles wide at its narrowest point. The bulk of Israel's population lived within artillery range of hostile Arab armies. I am not about to ask Israel to live that way again." The United States stands firmly behind that solemn commitment.

If Israel and the United States continue to work together, we can make progress toward peace.

The Economic Challenge

We know that peace is essential to Israel's security. But there is another important element to that security. The strength of Israel also depends on the strength of its economy. Israel must work to overcome its economic problems. Because of our own deep interest in a strong, healthy, and secure Israel, we will also do our part in ways we can be most helpful.

We in America know what it is like to live through difficult economic times. Only in the past three years have we begun to pull ourselves out of the spiraling stagflation of the late 1970s. We also know how hard it is to make the tough political decisions and the sacrifices needed to put an economy on a stable path of growth without inflation. We know firsthand how tough it is to cut the budget. Yet these tough decisions must be made.

But remember, the Israeli economy is a spectacular success story. The Israeli standard of living has risen steadily and remarkably. Israeli goods compete successfully in the major international markets. In fact, in 1984 Israel increased its exports by about 12.5 percent, while simultaneously reducing its imports by 2.5 percent. If the United States had done the same in percentage terms, our trade deficit would be more than $80 billion lower than it is today.

Still, the Israeli economy faces real problems. Israel is consuming more than it produces, and its economy is beset by a large national debt, untenable budget deficits, structural rigidities, and powerful inflationary forces. There are no quick solutions to these problems—yet Israelis have proved during the state's early decades that they could pull together to build and maintain a dynamic, growing economy. Israel has all the qualities needed for economic success: an educated, dynamic people; impressive capacities for research and development of new technologies; and outstanding universities. Israel's economic achievements in previous years were a testament to the public spirit, bravery, creativity, and talents of its people. I have no doubt that those same qualities today hold out the promise of future prosperity.

But Israel must pull itself out of its present economic trauma. And the Israeli people must do it themselves; no one can do it for them. Israel will need support as it makes the needed adjustments, and here the United States can and must help. But our help will be of little avail if Israel does not take the necessary steps to cut government spending, improve productivity, open up its economy, and strengthen the mechanisms of economic policy. Israel and its government must make the hard decisions. Prime Minister Peres and Finance Minister Modai have shown courageous leadership; they deserve support, here and in Israel, for this effort.

From 1981 to 1984, the United States provided almost $9.5 billion in aid to Israel. In 1984, aid to Israel made up more than a quarter of our entire foreign aid program. Yet we must all understand that this aid cannot really help unless Israel makes hard and far-reaching decisions for structural adjustment.

The United States can also help Israel in other ways, over the long term, to achieve the economic success Israel is capable of achieving. Tomorrow, for instance, the United States and Israel will formally sign the Free Trade Area Agreement. This will guarantee Israel completely open access to the world's largest and most diverse market. So, when you say to an investor, "What can be the market for what you're doing?" the Free Trade Area Agreement provides guaranteed access to the biggest and most diverse market there is. It's a very important development. In 1983, the United States imported almost $1.5 billion worth of Israeli products. The Free Trade Area Agreement will strengthen our trade partnership even further.

And we have created a Joint Economic Development Group for a continuing dialogue on the problems of the Israeli economy and on ways that our cooperation can help.

The future belongs to the free, the venturesome, the educated, and the creative. The Israeli people are all of these. Their future is bright.

America's Pledge

In the years to come, Israel and the United States will stand together in defense of our shared values and in support of our common goals. Our two peoples have the same vision of a better world—a world of peace and freedom, where the dignity of all men and women is respected by all nations. The evils we see all around us today—terrorism and the states that sponsor it, the persecution of Jews and other minorities in the Soviet Union, the outrages against Israel in the United Nations—these only strengthen our determination.

Every year thousands of Americans visit Yad Vashem, the memorial to the victims of the Holocaust. I will go there again next month. The images of Jewish suffering at Nazi hands still burn in our memories. Our pledge at the end of World War II was simple: never again. And our support for Israel is the lasting embodiment of that pledge.

Our two nations know that eternal vigilance is, indeed, the price of liberty. The world will be safe for decency only if men and women of decency have the courage to defend what they cherish. Security and strength are the foundation of survival—and of any serious foreign policy. They are essential not only for the defense of liberty but for any hopes for peace. Those who would threaten peace and freedom must know that the champions of peace and freedom stand strong and united.

America and Israel have learned this lesson. Together, we will set an example for all free people: we will work tirelessly for peace and for a better world.

WHAT I LEARNED ABOUT ISRAEL

Address delivered in San Francisco on October 12, 2017.

When I was a dean at the University of Chicago, we always had a special reception for the students who made the dean's list. Always present were Josef Levy and his wife. Of course, Josef was smart, but I could see that there was something special about him. I thought, "This kid is going somewhere." I had barely heard that the Six-Day War had started when I got the news that Josef had been killed. His wife was pregnant at the time.

I learned three things about Israel from this experience:

1. High human talent is there.
2. Its citizens are extraordinarily patriotic.
3. They live in a lousy neighborhood.

On a trip to Israel in 2016, Josef Levy's widow, his son, and his son's wife met with me at the King David Hotel. The constant refrain from Levy's son was, "Tell me about my father. I never knew my father." We then went to the outskirts of Jerusalem, where a memorial honoring their heroism had been built on the place where Josef Levy and six fellow soldiers had fallen during the war. That night, Prime Minister Benjamin Netanyahu hosted a dinner in my honor. He invited Josef Levy's widow and son to attend and asked them to stand for a round of applause. That day strongly reinforced my view about the Israelis' talent, patriotism, and lousy neighborhood.

* * *

In July 1969, as secretary of labor, I went to Israel as a guest of Israel's labor secretary. We were both struggling with the problem of bringing people with distinct disadvantages into the labor force. While there, I was somehow fortunate enough to spend an evening with Teddy Kollek, who showed me around Jerusalem. It was an unforgettable night. There were parties everywhere. Many different groups were having a good time.

Then he took me to his office, where I realized that he was teaching me something. I remember Teddy explaining to me, "Jerusalem is a beautiful city, but you have to understand it." He said, "Think of a painting. In most paintings, the colors are blended. But in Jerusalem, there are many different categories of Jews and Arabs, among other groups. So you have to think of Jerusalem as a mosaic, and the job of the mayor is to make the mosaic into a beautiful picture." You must let the diversity express itself but also give them something that pulls them together.

That's the way he thought of his job. It was a beautiful, interesting image. Teddy and I became friends, and he visited here a couple of times. On another occasion, he gave me the Jerusalem Medal. The ceremony took place in his office, and there were twenty-five or thirty people there—some Jews, some Arabs, and so on—and that was part of his mosaic imagery. I think he was very farsighted because, in the information and communication age, an urgent problem is learning how to govern over diversity. Teddy showed us how to do it.

* * *

When I was secretary of state, the Israeli prime minister and the foreign minister would visit from time to time. They were understandably preoccupied with security issues. But I had been looking at their economy and warned them to pay attention. This was not their priority until 1983–84, when Israel was hit with hyperinflation. They came to me and said, "You warned us, so now tell us what we should do." I talked with my friend Milton Friedman and others, and we developed a program and made a deal with Congress, the Israeli government, and the American Jewish community. The deal was that I would be the "heavy," blamed for any problems that might emerge. The other side of the deal was that the Israelis would do what I said. All this changed after considerable turmoil in Israel, as Peres succeeded Shamir as prime minister.

I persuaded two talented economists, Herb Stein and Stan Fischer, to work with me on these issues. Herb and Stan worked the ideas and the people and helped bring about the softest landing from hyperinflation on record. Stan later became the central banker for Israel and did an absolutely superb job.

I learned in that process that there were plenty of problems in the Israeli economy. My friend Max Fisher, a major Detroit industrialist, gathered some friends and told me that he planned to go to Israel to establish various corporate presences and trade relations that would help the Israeli economy. He came back some weeks later with his tail between his legs. He said, "I said to the prime minister, 'When you ask a guy like me to give money to Israel, I give. But when you ask me, an experienced businessman, to make investments in Israel, I ask questions. I'm not getting any answers, so I'm not going to invest.'" Obviously, more work needed to be done.

When Benjamin Netanyahu became finance minister, I had this experience on my mind as Bibi asked for advice. There were some good Israeli economists there who had studied in the United States, and we suggested that he get them on his team. He did a spectacular job of loosening up the regulatory shackles on the Israeli economy. Now it is thriving.

It also became clear that the Israeli government needed to have a real budget. A nominal budget existed, but no one paid attention to it. Government agencies just spent what they wanted to spend. Arye Carmon and Bernie Marcus asked me to join them in creating the Israel Democracy Institute (IDI), an organization dedicated to maintaining democracy in a country surrounded by hostility. I accepted, and during a long meeting in my conference room at the Hoover Institution, I said we should try to do something about the budget. Arye went to work with skill and enthusiasm and produced what is known as the Caesarea Process. A budget was put together with a broad base of support that involved buy-in by various elements of the Israeli government. The budget now has meaning, thanks to IDI.

I learned from all this that classic economic principles work. The money supply is key to price stability. Too heavy a regulatory hand can stifle even a relatively lively economy like that of Israel. Any key process in government, or for that matter, any large organization, does best when the result comes from a participatory process that produces buy-in from all participants.

* * *

I've often been asked what was the most satisfying development in my time as secretary of state. People expect me to say it was having a hand in bringing the Cold War to an end. That was a high point, but what government service is all about is helping people.

I worked hard and consistently on the problem of Soviet Jewry, often going to Israel before Moscow to buttress my credentials. I met, whenever I went to Moscow, many dissidents. Among them was a woman named Ida Nudel. There was a sense of hopelessness, with one person standing against a heavy state apparatus, but I always took inspiration from the courage of the Jews who were refuseniks. They stood up for what they believed, no matter what. These courageous Jews were not classic protesters. What they wanted was the freedom to worship and emigrate to the friendly environments of Israel and the United States. I put Ida Nudel's name on a list and gave it to Eduard Shevardnadze, and he promised to look into each case on the list. Our mantra was "NEVER GIVE UP."

One afternoon, the phone rang in my State Department office. I picked up the phone, and a small voice on the other end said, "This is Ida Nudel. I'm in Jerusalem. I'm home." That was a high point for me as secretary of state. Of course, it was satisfying to see the mass exodus of Jews to Israel and the United States as the situation in the Soviet Union loosened up under the guidance of Mikhail Gorbachev. But I learned from this experience that if you are onto something important for humanity, even though the situation looks bleak, NEVER GIVE UP.

Of course, Ida Nudel was not alone. Part of never giving up is doing something that is very visible.

When I visited Moscow in April 1987, I took part in a seder with well-known refuseniks in attendance. The meeting was publicized in advance, so I was given a few things to pass on to attendees, such as a photograph of a grandchild who might never be seen in person by his grandparents. The event was moving for everyone. I shook hands all around and we spent some time talking and praying. The idea was to do something to encourage people who were in a very difficult situation. The impact was very much the other way around. These people were really inspiring. They were individual Jews standing up for their own beliefs despite a big, omnipresent, and cruel state. How could you not be inspired?

The next day, I had a meeting with General Secretary Gorbachev in the Kremlin. He criticized me, saying, "Why are you always meeting with those lousy Jews?" referring to the refuseniks. I said, "Have I got a deal for you. I have a large airplane on the tarmac. If you want to get rid of those lousy Jews, put them on my plane and I will take them to a place where they will be welcomed." He changed the subject.

The message is clear and broad: Stand up for what you believe in and never give up.

* * *

In 1985, we saw a chance to bring Jordan and Israel together. King Hussein seemed ready to talk, but he kept insisting on an international umbrella under which talks could take place. We were planning a big event in connection with Gorbachev's visit to Washington. We thought this would be a terrific umbrella for King Hussein and expected that the Israelis would welcome the opportunity.

I pitched the idea to President Reagan and he agreed, but with conditions. He said, "First, go to the Israelis. If they agree, then go to King Hussein. If he agrees, then go to Gorbachev. If he agrees, we can go ahead."

There was a shared government in Israel at that time. Shimon Peres was foreign minister, and I went to him first. Peres agreed but would not say anything. He thought that if he said yes publicly, Shamir would immediately say no. He said, "I won't say anything, but you have me in your pocket."

Shamir said he would think it over and give me his decision the next day. My day was spent at the Weizmann Institute, so our meeting took place that evening. I had also organized a private dinner with Shamir to discuss Soviet Jewry. As I was leaving for dinner, one of my staff said, "The evening will either be short or very long." I asked what he meant. He said, "If he says no, it will be a short evening. If he says yes, we will be up very late writing MOUs, side letters, and so on."

I went off to dinner, and Yitzhak and I had a good talk about Soviet Jewry. The meeting came, and it was time for Shamir to speak. He said, "Mr. Secretary, you know our dreams, and you know our nightmares. We trust you. Go ahead." That was it. No MOU, no side letters. I learned once again the tremendous importance of trust in any relationship. Trust is the coin of the realm in dealing with others on whatever subject. If there is no trust, there will be no good deals.

* * *

Our biggest problem with Israel during the Reagan administration involved some excessively adventurous intelligence officials. The US Iran-Contra episode started as an Israeli idea. The aim was to somehow overcome Iran's alienation from the United States and, ultimately, Israel. After many years of good relations under the shah, Iran was, after the 1979 revolution, a major problem for both the United States and Israel. The idea was to change Iran's attitude by selling them arms with which to fight Saddam. We would get Hezbollah to release American and other hostages in Lebanon. The Israeli idea was peddled to the United States secretly through the NSC [National Security Council] staff at the White House. They got President Reagan on board by hitting a soft spot: release of US hostages. The trade of arms for hostages was a terrible idea, exposing US citizens abroad to peril by exhibiting a willingness to trade for their release. This whole process gradually unraveled into what became known as the Iran-Contra affair, the worst time of the Reagan presidency.

When Secretary of Defense Caspar Weinberger and I found out about this secret process, we both opposed it vigorously, but by that time, the president was hooked.

So something that started as an Israeli idea imploded, but we can't just blame Israel. We did not have to buy their idea.

The other problem was caused by Israel's acceptance of Jonathan Pollard's offer to be a spy. This was a serious mistake that set back relations. Shimon Peres called me and apologized, promising full cooperation. The United States went ahead and applied its legal processes.

Nations will inevitably, from time to time, have problems with each other. We have had differences with Israel. The measure of a truly committed relationship is whether it can deal effectively with the challenges that arise, and continue to thrive. Our relationship with Israel, we all learned, is easily strong enough to overcome the ill-considered plans of our intelligence services.

* * *

Some years ago, in the spring of 2010, I was in Israel, staying in a nice suite in the King David Hotel. Salam Fayyad, who was then prime minister of the Palestinian Authority, came to see me and told me about efforts he was leading to build up an economy on the West Bank and to create some institutional arrangements and systems of government. The Israelis, he said, were helping a lot but not visibly. Whatever good happened, the credit would go to Fayyad and the Palestinians.

Then I met with US Army Lt. Gen. Keith Dayton, who said, "My job is to create a Palestinian gendarme, an organized police force, on the West Bank." Well, how do you go about that? Where do you get the people? He says, "Well, the Palestinians nominate them." So then what happens? "Then we vet them." Then what happens? "The Israelis vet them, but nobody's supposed to know that the Israelis vet them, but everybody wants to be sure the Israelis vet them"—in other words, a very sophisticated process. "Then the Jordanians train them and they vet them. Then they come back and they're ready." I said, "Well, they have arms. Where do they get the arms?" "The Israelis supply the arms, but nobody's supposed to know that the Israelis supply the arms but everybody knows the Israelis supply the arms."

So here are the Israelis training and equipping a Palestinian police force—exactly the opposite of Gaza—because they see that between Fayyad's approach and the Dayton effort, it might just be possible to create something that provides a stable way of life in the West Bank. In the process, you build a Ministry of Interior supporting infrastructure and an ongoing capacity for senior leadership training. And if you can do all that, what you do is you grow, in effect, a functioning state. And then you have something you might someday be able to recognize.

Put these two things together and let them evolve, and something important will develop. There will be a sense of pride in a governing setup that works.

The minute you try to negotiate a so-called two-state solution, you divide people. A seemingly endless failure of that effort emphasizes differences and how difficult they are to resolve. So I say: Let's get back to what Fayyad and Dayton were doing—with Palestinians in the lead but with the total, but invisible, support of the Israelis.

* * *

Over a long period of time, I have had the privilege of lots of contact with Israel and with Israelis. Taking it all together, I see very clearly a flow of high human talent and patriotism that are practically instinctive. Israelis still live in a tough neighborhood. The violence in Iraq and Syria is extreme, and there is the constant threat posed by Iran, now enabled by money and access as a result of the nuclear deal. At the same time, an interesting shift is taking place in that the Sunni Arab states now look on Israel as more of an ally than an enemy. So the violence remains, but the sands of the Middle East are changing.

Israel's response to these pressures: maintaining a thriving democracy, making as many friends as it can, but also being able to defend itself. History is always present, and the memory of the Holocaust is never lost.

I also watched the Israeli economy transform from government dominance to one that relies on economic basics: monetary and fiscal policy, a budget that has real meaning, and a relatively gentle regulatory approach. So it seems that Israel has a thriving economy.

I have also come to see, on a global basis, that the problem of governing over diversity is a central issue. There was a time when diversity could be ignored or suppressed, but in this information and communication age, that is increasingly difficult to do. The lessons I learned about this problem from Teddy Kollek remain. He understood the diversity of Jerusalem and the need to let it operate. He also learned the importance of providing an overarching theme—in this case, the Golden Dome of Jerusalem.

Everybody, it seems, gets enamored of potential negotiations—dreaming about a two-state solution resulting in Israel and a Palestinian state living peacefully side by side. I have come to see that negotiations inevitably invite identifying things the different sides disagree about, and since negotiations between Israel and the Palestinians have historically failed, doing something about these differences is very difficult.

In my exposure to the work being done by former Palestinian prime minister Salam Fayyad and Lt. Gen. Dayton of the US Army, I saw they were creating working arrangements on economic and government institutions and security forces. Their initiatives strike me as a much better way to go. If you wind up with workable living arrangements, then maybe something significant will come of it.

When all is said and done, there is one idea that comes back to me wherever I go and with whomever I deal. That is the importance of developing relationships of trust where you can have candid conversations, knowing that those conversations will not be betrayed, and knowing that promises will be kept. So, remember one thing: trust is the coin of the realm. We will continue to learn from and help Israel so long as our trust in each other remains strong.

CHAPTER 3

A Changing World

CHAPTER 3

A Changing World

Our modern world is set to be transformed by emerging, twenty-first-century technologies. The means of production are also changing rapidly. Artificial intelligence and automation are empowering new machines capable of learning and adapting to new environments. Advanced manufacturing, especially robotics and 3-D printing, is changing how we make things but also what we can make. Goods can increasingly be made on demand, near where they are consumed. These new technologies will have serious consequences for the workforce. Employers and employees alike will have to adjust. They also threaten to level the international security environment, diffusing power to smaller states and nonstate actors.

Meanwhile, the rapid spread of information and constant communications is breaking down old barriers, allowing people to know what's going on and to organize even across continents. This is making the problem of governance even harder.

This issue has lately been at the forefront of my mind. The first essay in this chapter—a piece I wrote in 2018 for the *Wall Street Journal*—lays out the challenges these technological advances pose for governance. As I wrote then, these changes are happening, but what's more important is the speed with which they're happening. And that's something we have to better understand.

And while much is new, the basic problem of adjusting to change is old. The sewing machine, to take just one example, revolutionized the clothing industry. Its productivity was such that a sewing machine–employing garment factory set up by one early French inventor in the 1830s was sacked by angry Parisian tailors. Isaac Singer later improved the machine and sold it widely at a price equal to one-fifth of average American annual incomes; despite the price, he sold enough to die a very rich man. The *New York Times* wrote in 1860:

> The application of machinery to the purposes of sewing is of recent date, yet it has quietly worked its way into a position of great importance, not only in the relief that it brings to thousands of needle-women, but in a commercial view. . . . The use of the sewing-machine has already become far more extensive than the most sanguine anticipated. . . . The sewing upon a gentleman's shirt can be accomplished with ease in one hour upon a first-class sewing machine. It would take 14 hours of close and weary application to do the same by hand. . . . Every day extends their use into remoter parts of the country and of the world.[6]

Likewise in farming. In the 1880s, over half of the US labor force was employed in agriculture. One hundred years later, that figure was just over 3 percent. And today it is half that again. This change came alongside fundamental improvements in the technological productivity of farming: mechanization, animal and plant breeding improvements, and farm consolidation. It transformed American rural life. Those who remained in agriculture become more efficient, while many of their children moved to cities. Today, farm household incomes exceed the US national average, whereas they used to fall below it. And food costs as a share of overall American spending fell dramatically too, benefiting urban consumers.

We can learn from the past. In the early 1950s, I was a young professor in the MIT Department of Economics, and

by 1955 I got an early impression of the sorts of policy problems considered in Washington when I joined President
Dwight Eisenhower's Council of Economic Advisers.

At the time, American factories were modernizing, with
heavy investment in capital alongside a rapidly expanding
economy. Of course, like today, people were worried about the
impact of these new technologies on jobs: would factory
workers be replaced by machines and "electronic brains"? A
colleague and I talked about these emerging topics during our
daily carpools back and forth from the MIT campus, and we
eventually organized them into this essay on automation. It
could almost have been written today.

AMERICA CAN RIDE THE 21ST CENTURY'S WAVES OF CHANGE

Originally published in the Wall Street Journal *on June 28, 2018.*

The world is experiencing change of unprecedented velocity and scope. Governments everywhere must develop strategies to deal with this emerging new world. They should start by studying the forces of technology and demography that are creating it.

Change is the raw material of history. What gnaws at me now is the speed of change. In the last century, machines performed as instructed. Today, they can be designed to learn from experience, by trial and error. This will improve productivity—but it will also accelerate workplace disruption.

Societies usually had time to adjust to economic revolutions. In the early twentieth century, American farmworkers fell from half the population to less than 5 percent as agriculture was mechanized. We were able to establish a public school system to retrain those workers' children for jobs in the cities. But today, the rapid destruction of old jobs and simultaneous creation of new ones means that the workers themselves must adapt.

There are now 6.7 million "unfilled jobs" in America. Filling them with new and newly displaced workers will test both education (particularly K–12, where the United States continues to fall behind) and the flexibility of workers to pursue new occupations. Community colleges and similar institutions can help, on a time scale more attuned to new technology's rapidity. They deserve strong support.

Another force of change that needs to be understood more fully is the information and communications revolution, which is making governance more difficult. Information is everywhere—some of it accurate, some of it deliberately inaccurate. We have ceaseless and instantaneous communication to everybody, anybody, at any time. People can easily find out what is going on, organize around it, and take collective action—and they do.

Autocrats respond by using the same technology for surveillance and repression, as they try to govern this new form of diversity by suppressing it. Democracies have too often become trapped in short-term reactions to the vocal interests that most effectively capture governance infrastructures. Both responses have produced sharp declines in trust toward institutions. In the long run, neither will work.

Fundamental changes in the technological means of production will furthermore allow goods to be produced on demand, near where they will be used, in ways that can unsettle international order. Sophisticated use of robotics alongside human colleagues, plus 3-D printing and unexpected changes in the distribution of energy supplies, have implications for our security and economy.

Similar manufacturing advances also diffuse military power—through ubiquitous sensors, inexpensive and autonomous drones, high-powered nanoexplosives, and less costly access to space through microsatellites. These developments empower smaller states and even individuals, eroding incumbent powers like the United States of their current advantage. We will increasingly need to be vigilant that our words and deeds aren't revealed to be backed by empty threats.

Against this, the world's population is undergoing its own dramatic reordering just as emerging technologies hint at a potential new deglobalization.

In developed countries, fertility is decreasing as life expectancy is increasing. This reduces the working-age population and increases the cost of pensions and care for the elderly—requiring government budgets that increasingly crowd out other productive investments. The populations of many of today's major powers—Japan, Germany, Russia, even China—are set to shrink. Notably this isn't the case for the United States, Canada, and Australia, all countries with a long history of immigration. Will these trends continue?

In developing South Asia and in Africa, however—where most of the growth in world population comes from—persistently high fertility rates aren't sufficiently matched by economic growth. These regions also feel a disproportionate impact from natural disasters, human and agricultural diseases, and resource scarcities. That disparity underlies the global movement of peoples, setting off a populist turn in world politics.

So what should we do about all this? We should think local and global. Technology and demography can't be halted; they will always go forward. The United States will need to find ways to adapt domestically, but if these trends are handled well, the prospects for America to benefit are remarkably bright. I think in particular of how the Founders addressed the problem of governance through their own time of change by leaning on the diversity of individual states and localities—governments whose ears were closer to the ground, so that they were more nimble.

Meanwhile, America's allies and adversaries are likely to struggle with many of these changes, more than the United States will. America's own global leadership will face growing demands. The more we can understand other countries' situations, the stronger our foundation for constructive national and international engagement will be.

The twenty-first century's waves of change are being driven by technology, not by the humanities. But to move beyond these disruptions, we have to think through this change in human terms.

AUTOMATION: A NEW DIMENSION TO OLD PROBLEMS

George P. Shultz and George B. Baldwin

Originally published in the Annals of American Economics, *Public Affairs Press, Washington, DC, 1955. Edited for length.*

Automation is certainly one of the most talked-about forms of technological change to come down the pike in a long time. Too often, however, it is not a development that people study and discuss sensibly, but an issue around which they choose up sides. This is hardly surprising, for automation is a new and somewhat mysterious development, one that may affect large areas of our economy, and it is still sufficiently unformed and uncertain in its impact that some people view it as a major threat to their security. There are many others, of course, who welcome automation with open arms, seeing it as an exciting new kind of technological progress that will rapidly raise our standard of living and give us not only more income but more leisure time as well.

It is perfectly possible that both the pessimists and the optimists are right: automation does indeed pose a threat to some people's security, and it will also speed up the rise in our standard of living. But in our view the benefits will far outweigh the injuries—particularly if people understand what automation is, how fast it may spread, and how to deal with its more threatening aspects. Our purpose here is to reduce the amount of controversy surrounding automation and to add something to an understanding of it. But do not expect to find all the answers about automation in this paper—or indeed anywhere else today: the future impact of automation, like the future generally, is uncertain. This means that we need to remain flexible in our thinking and in our social institutions so that we can make the best use of the opportunities for change that automation will create.

What Is Automation?

Today, people are calling every conceivable kind of technological change "automation." This is riding fashion too hard, because there are still thousands of technological changes occurring every week that have nothing at all to do with automation. The term is not a synonym for technological change: it is instead a particular kind of technological change that has gathered momentum since the Second World War.

How does automation differ from other types of technological change? One important difference is this: most forms of technological change, like the development of automatic bottle-blowing machines or coal-cutting machinery, are specific to a single industry in their application. Automation, on the other hand, stands for a *generalized* form of technological change, one potentially applicable over a wide range of manual and white-collar operations in a great many industries. In this sense, it promises to have an impact like that of mass production—another great general principle that has transformed the nature of the manufacturing process (and of many business practices) during the past two generations.

Automation is really much more complicated than we have so far suggested. One of the most common mistakes in much of our current thinking about automation is to regard it solely as a technological phenomenon. True enough, it is primarily a technological development. But in a more abstract sense it consists of a new way of thinking about the total process of production; it forces us to think in new ways about the total conduct of a business, including those operations that occur outside the plants and offices of a firm. The key to this new perspective is flow or continuous process, in contrast to intermittent or stop-and-go methods. Where technology permits, many products can be made at lower cost, in greater volume, and often with higher quality when they are made with a continuous rather than an intermittent method of manufacture. Automation is basically a technological development that allows us to realize this flow principle more perfectly.

It allows this because it consists of a distinctive set of technological changes that touch the production process at points which have previously lain outside the reach of other kinds of technological change. In this sense it is true that automation is primarily a technological development. But it also has characteristics that will force us to reexamine the total business process (including pricing policy, product mix, market research and marketing methods, product design, and so on) and not just machine design, shop layout, and production scheduling. More conventional technological changes rarely reach beyond the manufacturing process itself, and usually not beyond narrow parts of that. These secondary business implications, which grow out of the primary technical dimension of automation, have major implications for the managerial skills our economy will need.

So far so good: but what *is* the technological nature of automation? The most important fact here is that its technical dimension is not unitary or simple: automation is a family of several quite different technical developments. Nevertheless, there seem to be three major developments that, taken together, account for nearly everything that comes under the heading of automation. These three fundamental developments are:

1. The linking together of conventionally separate manufacturing operations into lines of continuous production through which the product moves "untouched by human hands." This first development, which depends primarily on mechanical engineering for its adoption, we shall refer to simply as *integration*, a term already in wide use in the metalworking industries. It is also called *Detroit automation* in honor of the industry in which it got its start. *Continuous automatic production* is another and perhaps more descriptive term being used.

2. The use of "feedback" control devices or servomechanisms, which allow individual operations to be performed without any necessity for human control. With feedback, there is always some built-in automatic device for comparing the way work is actually being done with the way it is supposed to be done and then automatically making

any adjustments that may be necessary in the work process. This second development we shall refer to simply as "feedback" technology; it is dependent primarily not on mechanical but on electrical engineering knowledge and techniques.

3. The development of general and special purpose computing machines capable of recording and storing information (usually in the form of numbers) and of performing both simple and complex mathematical operations on such information. We shall refer to this aspect of automation as "computer technology," a technology that rests primarily on new developments in electrical engineering.

Integration developments have the primary effect of eliminating the need for labor devoted to materials handling, including the functions of exact machine loading and unloading. *Feedback* automation has the primary effect of eliminating the need for labor devoted to controlling the performance of operations between the time when the work is set in place and when it is finished—that is, gauging the work and adjusting the machine or machines. The third embodiment of automation, the *computer,* is not only of enormous value in solving difficult mathematical problems presented by scientific and engineering research but is also capable of handling a large number of the traditional office operations characteristic of banks, insurance companies, payroll departments, and the like.

We have seen integration used alone, feedback used alone, computers used alone, and all three used in various combinations. For example, the Cleveland Engine Plant of Ford Motor Company relies almost exclusively on the integration concept. The notable engineering feature of the plant is the way separate operations are tied together by ingenious mechanical linkages that load and unload the production machines without human intervention. But few of the production machines in this plant employ the feedback principle in their operation; instead, they are programmed or scheduled to perform their operations a certain number of times (determined chiefly by tool wear) at the end of which a man must come and change the tool. But no man has to watch the machine while it operates.

If the production machines themselves had built-in electronic devices that adjusted the machines' performance to compensate for tool wear without any persons changing the tool or adjusting the machine, we would speak of feedback. An example of feedback and computers used in combination is MIT's automatic milling machine, which cuts out complex metal shapes by following instructions programmed into the machine by means of holes punched in a paper tape. The holes are coded in such a way that they can be read by a computing machine called a "director," which in turn tells the milling machine itself what to do (a separate feedback system built into the milling machine makes sure it does exactly what the director has told it to do).

Lest it be thought that we are talking only of the "hardware" industries, we should point out that the feedback principle has probably been used most extensively in the petroleum and chemical process industries, whose raw materials are liquids. The concept of the completely automatic factory depends on various combinations of the three basic types of automation we have described above. However, we have found it more misleading than helpful to think in terms of the automatic factory, which does not seem likely to become a practical proposition in the manufacturing industries within the foreseeable future.

How Revolutionary Is the Development?

Some people think automation will have such far-reaching effects that they call it a second Industrial Revolution. A "revolution" is both a hopeful and a fearful image. To some, the word means a general upheaval that suddenly throws into confusion accustomed patterns of life and dispossesses large numbers of people. In our view, it is misleading to put this kind of alarmist interpretation on the kind of revolution brought by automation. Nothing so fast, so pervasive, or so disrupting is likely to come out of this development—and one of the main reasons it will not is because we lack the manpower skills to propel the changes at high speed even if we wanted to do so, as we might in a war. In any case, automation will not require anything like the large-scale geographical and sociological readjustments that were at the heart of the first Industrial Revolution, when an agricultural and rural population became industrialized and urbanized.

There is, however, a different sense in which automation can be called revolutionary. As the first Industrial Revolution gave men radically new forms and applications of *energy* and *power,* this second Industrial Revolution promises to provide them with radically new methods for exercising *control* over processes and operations. Indeed, automation not only gives us new ways of controlling existing processes but gives us wholly new forms of control that allow us to do things we could not do before. It will allow us to make some products we could not make before (certain types of chemical products, for example) and to perform some operations we could not perform before—such as gathering and analyzing desirable business information quickly and accurately enough to provide a sound factual basis for many critical business decisions.

This control function, where it involves the notion of feedback and the use of computers, has arisen out of a general theoretical breakthrough in the analysis of what information is and how it can be handled or processed. The new field of communications theory and research has grown up in close company with critical developments in the applied field of electrical engineering, the seminal invention being the development of the vacuum tube following World War I.

World War II greatly stimulated this work in communications theory and the development of electronic machines built around devices for controlling the flow of electrons and handling data in incredibly large quantities at unbelievably fast speeds. The commercial development of data-processing machines has gone forward very rapidly during the past six or seven years until today there are on the market several types of "electronic brains," or computers, which can be built to perform a remarkably wide range of operations that use numbers or letters as their primary raw material. We have all heard of Remington Rand's UNIVAC and

IBM's 600 or 700 series. Many other companies are rapidly developing both general and special purpose data-processing machines.

These complementary advances in communications theory and electronics provide the basis for significant new forms of technological change in both the office and the factory. However, the office changes are here and ready to go while the feedback- and computer-controlled factory seems to be approaching more slowly and with less certainty. The present examples of factory automation seem to be arising out of the integration process rather than out of feedback and computer applications. In the large office, the computer used alone is the dominant development. From what we have been able to observe to date, office automation is likely to come sooner and to proceed faster than factory automation.

There are three built-in brakes that tend to limit the spread of automation, hopefully to a pace that will not overtax our ability to absorb it without distress. These three governors are the technical limitations to the design of automation applications, the economic limitations of automation, and managerial ability to understand and take advantage of the opportunities that automation presents.

1. *Technical limitations*: Nearly all the automation applications one reads of today have been custom-designed, custom-made jobs. This is natural in view of the newness of the development, and it may be expected that engineers will accumulate design know-how at an increasing rate as they become more experienced, as the suppliers of components come to standardize their products, and as industry groups standardize their demands. But even granting increased standardization and an acceleration of engineering interest and competence in this field, we are still confronted by a general shortage of engineers, and particularly of those with the education and habits of mind conducive to the rapid extension of automation applications. Furthermore, automation requires not only new kinds of engineers but many more of them.

2. *The economics of automation*: One of the frustrations of creative engineers and designers is that many of their achievements turn out to be impractical for economic reasons. The field of automation is likely to abound in such examples. A lot of applications will be ruled out by the necessity for fairly stable product designs and the ability of the market to absorb a much higher volume of output. The design costs for automating production processes are often so high that they lie beyond the reach of all but the largest firms or smaller firms with government contracts. Perhaps most important is the limitation presented by the high capital costs of automation equipment, including high installation costs. These may often turn out to be so great that the product can be made more cheaply by present methods. In short, there may be many instances where automation, while technically feasible, just does not pay. We will rarely hear about such cases: we will hear about technological feasibility much more frequently than about the arithmetic of new investment opportunities that cannot be justified.

3. *Managerial imagination*: The third built-in brake on the rate of automation's speed will be the inability of many companies to identify and move in on automation opportunities as rapidly as the technology itself would permit them. This is said not in criticism of American management but simply because automation is likely to cause or require changes in business procedures and policies that will not be obvious and may involve more risk than the kind of technological change that stops on the factory floor. The skill bottleneck at the technical level is thus not the only brake; there is an equally important one at the managerial or decision-making level. Here is a field where qualities of imagination, entrepreneurship, and risk-taking will be important.

The factors just cited make it extremely unlikely that automation is going to race through our economy like a forest fire. But having entered this word of reassurance and caution, we do not want to leave the impression that automation is not a lusty and fast-stepping development likely to pick up speed as time goes on, or that we will not have important transition problems to face. And there are some important fields, such as the data-processing operations that now use large numbers of clerical employees, where automation technology is well advanced and new installations are likely to proceed just as fast as suppliers can deliver equipment and purchasers can train staffs to take advantage of the new technology. Here, fortunately, the process of eliminating clerical jobs can probably be handled by normal turnover, given good planning by management and labor groups and a continuation of tight labor market conditions in major metropolitan areas. . . .

Skills Required of the Labor Force

What will be the impact of automation on the abilities required of the labor force? Will it leave us with a predominance of dull, routinized jobs, where people are increasingly forced to conform to the dictates of the machine? Or is it more likely to open up jobs with greater intellectual challenge and to raise the skill composition of the labor force?

Any discussion of job mix is, of course, a discussion of proportions, of the relative weights of managerial, professional, skilled, semiskilled, and laboring jobs. Automation appears generally to bring about a change in the mix, so that the resulting weights tend to emphasize more highly skilled rather than less-skilled types of occupations. We have observed this upgrading effect in a limited number of cases, but the conclusion must rest more on logic than on proven statistical grounds. It seems reasonable to expect that the ratio of managers to employees will increase, in view of the increased value of the equipment for which an individual manager becomes responsible and of the increased proportion of the total work process inevitably brought under the supervision of one person. The value and complexity of the equipment similarly indicate a need for a higher proportion of engineers and, especially in the case of the electronic feedback and computer technologies, give rise to what amounts to a new occupation in most concerns, that of electronic technician.

In the factory, the new technology most readily takes over materials handling and completely routinized machine operations and tends to emphasize, as far as the average plant worker is concerned, jobs directed at "keeping the process going" because downtime becomes so costly. As one plant manager explained to us, "You can't afford to chase all over the factory for a maintenance man when something goes wrong. He's got to be right there, and he's got to know something about electrical and hydraulic problems, not just mechanical." So the proportion of maintenance people is likely to increase as well as the skills required of them. This is not to say that all routine or heavy jobs are eliminated or to overlook the fact that many skilled jobs may disappear or become less important quantitatively. But in terms of overall proportions, it seems likely that automation will have an upgrading effect on the job mix in those areas of the economy where it is employed. The conclusion may be further bolstered by reference to the oil and chemical industries, where automation has a relatively long history already.

There is at least one important qualification to be made in this picture: automation will not upgrade people; it will only upgrade jobs. This is a simple but vital distinction, for it highlights the crucial transition problems. If John Romano, a fifty-five-year-old grinder in Ford's crankshaft department, is put out of work by the introduction of an automated crankshaft machine, and George Pichelski's twenty-year-old boy decides to go to a school for electronic technicians instead of going to work as a drill press operator (and does in fact land a technician's job two years later at Chrysler), it is stretching language and compressing reality to say that a semiskilled operator has been upgraded into a highly skilled technician.

At any rate, the quantitative impact of automation on employment in those areas of our economy where it is used is almost impossible to estimate. Obviously, firms install the new equipment because it helps them reduce costs. While labor costs are not the only areas of savings, they are typically a major consideration. On the face of things, then, we would expect a reduction in employment opportunities, given some framework of total effective demand. But it is much easier to identify jobs that are being lost to technological change than those it is creating. Neglecting the possibility of greater demand for existing products resulting from lower prices, there is the virtual certainty that some wholly new products will be made technically or economically feasible by automation, particularly by the feedback control devices being developed. As an example of what we mean, it would be impossible to make some of the products that modern oil refineries now make without automatic controls. Thus the direct quantitative impact of automation presents at least an open question. Neither optimists nor pessimists can afford to be too dogmatic about long-run quantitative effects.

But suppose we assume that the industries where automation is used employ a smaller and smaller proportion of the labor force. Despite a direct effect of upgrading on the job mix, there might be a downgrading effect in the overall picture if the adjustments that take place are predominantly in unskilled occupations or in such areas as personal service. That seems to us unlikely, however. It seems as certain as any social trend can be that the demand for professional services, especially medical and educational, and the opportunities for self-employment in fields such as recreation, will increase rapidly during the next ten years and beyond. And with the higher standards of living made possible by technological advance, the adjustment may be made through a continuation of present trends toward longer vacations, more holidays, and a shorter work week. In that event, we may well see another long-term trend continued: a further reduction in the number of unskilled jobs and an increase in emphasis on the more skilled and professional occupations.

In short, our guess is that both the direct short-run and indirect longer-run effects of automation on employment will call for more and not less skill on the part of our labor force. We are entitled to a cautious hope that automation may afford a partial answer to those who look at the rising educational levels in the country and ask, "What are people going to do with all that education when they find themselves in the dull and routine jobs of American industry?" *Mechanization* may indeed have created many dull and routine jobs—but *automation* is a reversal, not an extension, of this trend: it promises to cut out just that kind of job and to create others of greater interest and higher skill. . . .

Implications for Education and Training

What are the implications of these skill and job changes for the kinds of education and training that people will need in the future? We see seven that we want to comment on briefly.

1. *Some new skills will be required—in the skilled manual, the technician, and the professional categories alike.* This assertion only states what is obvious; but it is worth stating because just what kinds of new skills will be required is far from clear, since the new technology itself is far from crystallized. In terms of training, this means that the identification and development of these new skills will have to occur at the cutting edge of the new technology, that is, in companies that have some experience with automation. From the viewpoint of education, it means that we need to think in terms of professional people who can design, and skilled people who can learn and operate, an unsettled and highly dynamic technology. We need school and college graduates with an imaginative and creative cast of mind, flexible and uncommitted in the ways they think about their jobs; it would be a great mistake if our educational institutions turned out people drilled to a state of proficiency in known and specialized arts. In terms of curricula, educators should think primarily of providing generalized and basic courses rather than specialized subjects that might enjoy current fashion. The strengthening of mathematics and the physical sciences, already a problem of some concern in American education, will serve the needs of automation well. At the

professional level, it is important for engineers and educators alike to realize that current developments in science shape tomorrow's engineering practice.

We have not said much about the effect of automation on the technician group, a small but rapidly expanding category of skilled manpower that requires some formal schooling beyond that generally received by the population at large. Automation may expand this group in two ways: (1) with its emphasis on electronics, on programming, on instrumentation and other precision operations, automation seems bound to create many new technician positions of a bona fide nature; but (2) automation may also create opportunities for redefining some redesigned jobs as "technician" positions, even though employees will not need the advanced schooling that a pure technician needs. There are oil refineries, for example, that have found some of their hourly operators' jobs so changed by automation that they have reclassified the jobs, put the workers on a salary, and found that a higher type of applicant applied for the jobs. By allowing some people to come to work in white collars instead of overalls, by substituting paperwork and observational functions for manual tasks, automation may upgrade the status of many people in addition to their skills.

2. *The main training responsibility must lie with individual companies, which can save time and money by learning from each other.* We have already made the point that the mapping of a frontier has to be done by people at the frontier. But it would be a frightful waste of money, time, and energies if the experience one company had accumulated in converting its workforce to automation was not made available to other companies wrestling with the same problems. Informal contacts and professional bodies will make some contribution to the exchange of necessary information here, but we think a much more fruitful way of making this experience available would be some fairly careful research

studies. The kind of studies we have in mind would serve as much more than a training aid, and we shall say something more about this suggestion below.

3. *Automation may also require the training of more people in some of the traditionally skilled manual occupations.* There *is* some evidence, which needs checking by further systematic research, that some firms converting to automation find they need more skilled trades than they needed before (there are other examples where just the opposite is true). Where automation does expand the number of skilled workers a company needs, a reexamination of the ways in which the company acquires its skilled employees may be in order just to make sure that the problem of numbers will be solved. In other words, automation may not only present a problem of new skills but, in some instances anyway, may lead to a quantitative increase in the demand for existing skills.

4. *The need for closer study of the traditional methods of acquiring skills.* One of the most significant facts to emerge from recent research on the skilled labor force is that well over half of our skilled manual workers pick up their skills outside of any formal training program. Work experience and informal training from supervisors and fellow workers are the main sources of skill formation. This means that promotion ladders, seniority systems, union rules, and labor market mobility are the key determinants of who has what opportunities to learn which skills. Apprenticeship and formal training programs will always be of great importance, but the extent to which we have recently come to recognize the role played by unorganized and informal practices suggests that companies which foresee a need for building a more skilled and more flexible workforce would do well to examine their informal shop practices and their negotiated shop rules, especially their seniority rules, to see how they affect the process of skill formation among their own employees.

5. *Adult education as a needed form of executive "training."* Automation should stimulate more companies to provide opportunities for their nonprofessional executives to stand back and take a reflective look at their own firms in particular and business practices in general. Several firms already send their executives, particularly their younger ones, to universities for refresher courses of varying kinds and for varying periods. A few hold weekend seminars of their own with invited lecturers from outside the company. In general, automation will expand the need for adult education among business managers, simply because continuing education is one way to keep good workers creative and flexible, qualities much needed by automation.

6. *The prospective increase in leisure time raises questions about the nature of our educational system.* In the long run, the most significant and revolutionary impact of automation and other forms of innovation may be on the opportunities we have to do something other than earn our living. We must certainly guard against orienting our educational system too much toward vocational objectives and too little toward the values of our culture and the higher pursuits of humanity.

7. *The best way to know what automation means for the work skills of the nation and to adjust our educational and training programs accordingly is to study it systematically.* We would have failed to make one of our major points if you do not sense that relatively few hard facts are known about the manpower as well as other implications of automation. One of the most useful research projects we can think of would be launching a modest series of rounded case studies of automation. We say "rounded" case studies, because there is much more to be learned about automation than merely its manpower implications, which take on much of their significance only within a larger context. What we have in mind are studies such as those organized by the

National Planning Association on the "Causes of Industrial Peace under Collective Bargaining" and those made
recently by the United States Department of Labor and
the Social Science Research Council on the mobility and
training of various segments of the labor force.

The Problem of Displacement

It would be silly to pretend that automation will not abolish many
jobs. Whether or not it creates, directly or indirectly, as many jobs
as it wipes out, no one knows. Despite uncertainty as to the speed
and scope of automation's impact, this much at least is certain:
there is bound to be a new influence at work that will strengthen
the arguments of those who feel that wage earners ought not bear
the main brunt of technological change.

Social shock absorbers such as severance pay, the guaranteed
annual wage, unemployment benefits, careful timing of labor-
saving innovations to coincide with business upswings, and additional information sharing between management and unions seem
likely to receive increased attention as automation spreads. If some
of these mobility benefits add to the cost of technological change,
that alone would not disturb us greatly. Indeed, it is important
to recognize clearly at least two types of costs incurred by the
displaced worker: (1) loss of income while finding a new job and
(2) loss of equities built up on the old job in the form of seniority,
pension rights, vacation rights, and so on. While unemployment
benefits of one kind or another are clearly a way of approaching the
first type of loss, the more general adoption of the severance pay
principle for people with substantial equities in existing jobs strikes
us as one entirely appropriate way to share some of the initial gains
involved. In addition, such gain sharing should strengthen the
hands of both management and union officials as they confront
the short-run pressures that inevitably develop whenever jobs are
threatened.

In developing policies to cushion the impact of automation,
just as with any major technological change, the toughest situa-

tions are not likely to be those in which some new machines and equipment are installed in a given plant; the toughest situations are likely to arise from competition between new plants designed for automation and older ones that are not. Sometimes the two plants will belong to the some company, sometimes not. In cases where automation expresses itself as competition among two or more firms not under common ownership, then the policies appropriate to it seem no different from those we would like to see in any competitive situation.

But when automation takes the form of changes internal to a particular firm, then management and unions have much greater control over the effects it will have and how these will be handled. For one outstanding characteristic of automation is that it takes time to install. Even after an exploratory stage has been completed, equipment must be designed and manufactured, men must be hired or trained for new occupations, physical installation and transition problems must be faced. All of this takes time—not days or weeks, but months or even years. And with problems like displacement and personal adjustment, time, of course, presents a major opportunity that alert and socially responsible companies and unions can use to good advantage. Social responsibility would mean telling new employees that their jobs were temporary, retraining old employees who have the requisite ability, permitting those near retirement to claim pension benefits, and so on.

We have already noted that automation is likely to have its greatest immediate impact on office occupations. In a sense, that is fortunate, since it will affect a class of worker for whom the blow can be softened most easily, namely female employees working in large offices. Not only is turnover markedly higher among female clerical employees, but the demand for them in recent years has been high in most labor markets. The most difficult adjustment problems in office automation are likely to concern the few longer-service employees (often men) who have built up career expectations around clerical supervisory positions that will be abolished as clerical groups are eliminated.

There is one further obvious point to be made. In considering the problem of the displaced and unemployed worker, it is not as important to ask why he lost his old job as how much trouble he has in getting a new one and what kind of new one he gets. This brings to the fore the educational and retraining problems to which we have already alluded. But even more, it serves to emphasize for an era of marked if not revolutionary change the importance of government economic policy directed toward the maintenance of "full employment." Change the level of unemployment by a few percentage points and the transition problems of displacement change from a relatively manageable question of adjustment to a social catastrophe of alarming proportions in which orderly technological progress becomes impossible.

Summary

We are not experts in automation, but we have tried to capture the meaning and the main implications of this new word that has found its way into everyone's vocabulary. In summary, these are our conclusions:

1. Automation is a form of technological change that puts renewed emphasis on thinking about a total and continuous process rather than the component parts of an intermittent process. Technically, it may involve continuous automatic materials handling, the automatic control of production operations through feedback systems, and revolutionary new means of processing and storing information (usually numbers).
2. It is a development certainly not confined to manufacturing in its possible range of applications; in fact, its greatest immediate impact may well be on office occupations and control functions such as scheduling, invoicing, and accounting.
3. The industrial relations problems associated with automation are broadly familiar to us all, as those commonly associated with any major technological or economic change. In some cases, these problems are given some-

what new dimensions; in any event, these problems remain a continuing challenge to our social and political ingenuity and our individual capacities for adjustment.

4. Among the opportunities presented by automation are those stemming from its likely effect on the skills required of our labor force and on the meaningfulness of individual jobs, which may well become more easily identified with a total process than has often been true in the past. While the need for skilled people is a problem from a personnel or recruiting point of view, in a broader sense it represents an opportunity for members of the labor force and a challenge to our educational and training abilities.

5. The major social problem connected with automation, displacement of labor, is almost certain to bring increased emphasis on means of cushioning the shock to workers and of retraining them to useful and satisfying economic roles in our society. In working toward these ends, we at least have the advantage that the introduction of automation typically involves considerable time between the initial decision to go ahead and the full-scale operation—time for company, union, and employees to plan and adjust, if they are adequately informed and provided with resources enough to get through the inevitable transition period. Of all the possible ways to share the gains from automation, we can think of none with a claim to higher priority.

I'm listening, George — I'm listening!
love Nancy

CHAPTER 4

The Drug Issue

I have been concerned about the drug issue since I became President Nixon's secretary of labor in 1969, when an informal effort was started to cut off the flow of addictive drugs to the United States. The thinking was this: drugs are bad for you, so let's make them unavailable so people have no ability to use them. This was a supply-oriented approach to the problem. Decades of sincere efforts to contain the drug supply, from military interdiction in international waters down to the beat cop on the street, followed.

But every administration since then has engaged in a war on drugs and lost. Drugs today remain plentiful and potent. One shipping container of synthetic fentanyl could supply the US illicit opioid market for a year; a package can be delivered from Shenzhen through the mail. Marijuana—perhaps more likely now to be ordered by iPhone than bought on a street corner—is four times more potent per dollar today than it was in the 1990s. It has become a $40 billion market. The war on drugs has exacted an immense cost but failed to achieve its objectives. Why haven't we held ourselves accountable for that failure and done something about it?

Many of our policy challenges today come down to technologies and society changing faster than governments have

Secretary of State George P. Shultz and First Lady Nancy Reagan following a speech on drug control at the United Nations on October 25, 1988.
COURTESY HOOVER INSTITUTION LIBRARY & ARCHIVES.

been able to respond. One in seven Americans now develop a substance abuse disorder in their lifetimes. More than one in four federal and state inmates reported committing their current offense while under the influence of illegal drugs. In drugs, too, we need to catch up.

Increasingly, we hear claims that the answer is legalization, especially for drugs argued to have some medical benefits, like marijuana. I can appreciate the motivations of these advocates, but they miss the point. Drugs are harmful, and our goal should be to get people to use them less, not more.

Drug legalization sends a message that drug use is okay. Rather, we should take a page from the tobacco control playbook: acknowledge that some people use drugs but nevertheless maintain a social and personal understanding that their broad use is harmful and should be avoided. So, as I suggested in my remarks at a 2011 symposium in honor of my good friend, the Nobel Prize–winning University of Chicago economist Gary Becker, consider the Portuguese model: keep the sale of drugs illegal but decriminalize use and possession of small amounts to free up government resources for more important antidrug activities elsewhere.

Today, state governors and now President Donald Trump are struggling with the opioid crisis. My advice is that they think about how to make our efforts to control drug demand as rigorous as those we have long employed toward supply.

Drug use starts as a personal problem, and much of our policy experimentation on the demand side of the equation has actually come from local levels—cities and states. These local experiences should be evaluated and the best programs supported.

The problem today is grim, but there is hope. The rate of cigarette smoking in the United States fell from 43 percent at the time of the 1964 US Surgeon General's Report to just 15 percent today, in large part due to the adoption of a gradual but consistent portfolio of approaches to make smoking less attractive. We should aim to do the same with other deleterious drugs by getting serious about demand.

Of course, economists are always thinking of supply and demand. The essays that follow show how my own thinking on this topic has developed over recent years alongside friends—economists themselves—who feel as strongly about this subject as I do.

GARY BECKER AND THE WAR ON DRUGS

Remarks delivered at the Symposium in Honor of Gary Becker's 80th Birthday, at the University of Chicago on February 11, 2011. Edited for clarity.

What should I talk about? I first went to my dog-eared copy of *The Essence of Becker*. The impact is tremendous. What a range of subjects! What crisp, clear, and compelling arguments! Then I looked over some blogs to get really up to date. All of this led me to my topic, which is "Gary Becker on the war on drugs and where he should go from here."

My reference points are three Becker blog posts: "The Failure of the War on Drugs" (March 20, 2005); "Response on Legalizing Drugs" (March 27, 2005); and "The American War on Drugs Is Not Only an American Disaster" (December 12, 2010); and a white paper for the Cato Institute by Glenn Greenwald, "Drug Decriminalization in Portugal: Lessons for Creating Fair and Successful Drug Policies" (April 2, 2009).[7]

Let me start by reviewing Gary's argumentation and then pose four questions that, as far as I can see, Gary has not addressed. So, my talk is a plea for more Becker on these questions.

About five years ago, Gary wrote a blog post titled "The Failure of the War on Drugs." The idea of the war is to reduce the use of drugs by limiting their supply. As Gary put it, "The war on drugs is fought by trying to apprehend producers and distributors of drugs, and then to punish them rather severely if convicted." He notes that "the expected punishment" causes the price to rise, and the economist in him says, "The higher price discourages purchase and consumption."

And then, in terms of the cost of the war: What's the price tag? He notes that the war has "increased the price of drugs by at least 200 percent" and explains why, but then his estimates move to direct costs (police, court time and effort spent on offenders, cost of imprisonment—a minimum of about $40,000 per year per prisoner). Gary quotes his own study with Kevin Murphy and Steve

Cicala, which estimated a cost of over $100 billion per year. He notes that this estimate doesn't include "intangible costs, such as the destructive effects on many inner city neighborhoods, the use of the American military to fight drug lords and farmers in Colombia and other nations, or the corrupting influence of drugs on many governments."

Then, in a blog post he wrote last December called "The American War on Drugs Is Not Only an American Disaster," Gary looks beyond the estimated US costs to examine the effects of the war on other countries—especially, right now, Mexico, and also Colombia, and other Latin American countries. He notes that "Mexico is engaged in a real war, with advanced military equipment used by the drug gangs; often the gangs have better weapons than the army does. The casualties have been huge." He says that major cities like Monterrey are hollowing out. As he notes, "No one has estimated the social cost of American drug policy on Mexico, Colombia, and other countries, but it has to be immense." All these costs are clearly very large—probably in excess of the earlier $100 billion. For the sake of easy, round numbers, let's call the total a cool quarter trillion a year.

Despite this immense cost, as Gary says in his March 20, 2005, blog post, "every American president since Nixon has engaged in a war on illegal drugs: cocaine, heroin, hashish, and the like. And every president without exception has lost this war." I want to put an exclamation point behind the word *lost*. Far from being successful in keeping drugs out of the United States, studies based on the World Health Organization's Composite International Diagnostic Interview, quoted in Glenn Greenwald's study, show the opposite: "A survey of 17 countries has found that despite its punitive drug policies, the United States has the highest levels of illegal cocaine and cannabis use."

The authors found that 16.2 percent of people in the United States had used cocaine in their lifetime, a level much higher than any other country surveyed (the second highest level of cocaine use was in New Zealand, where 4.3 percent of people reported having used cocaine). Cannabis use was also highest in the United States (42.4 percent), followed by New Zealand (41.9 percent).

The prevalence rate for cocaine usage in the United States was so much higher than the other countries surveyed that the researchers formally characterized it as an "outlier":

> The US was an outlier in lifetime cocaine use, with sixteen percent of respondents reporting that they had tried cocaine at least once compared to 4.0 to 4.3 percent in Colombia, Mexico, Spain, and New Zealand, and extremely low proportions in the Middle East, Africa, and Asia.

* * *

All this brings me to say that I agree with Gary's analysis, but he has not addressed, at least not so far as I know, the central question. In view of the immense costs—human as well as material—of the war on drugs and its complete failure to achieve its objectives, why haven't we done something about it?

Here the contrast with Prohibition is stark. Prohibition was put into effect in 1920 after the Eighteenth Amendment was ratified in 1919, and it produced results like the war on drugs. Thirteen years later, by the difficult process of another constitutional amendment (the Twenty-first Amendment), Prohibition ended. Why did we come to our senses on alcohol but can't do it on drugs? I'm hoping Gary will address that issue. Now, in my role as his research assistant, I'll give a few remarks to help him on his way.

Alcohol was deeply embedded in our society and, in many cases, not really frowned upon. There's the hook-'n-eye example. In the 1920s and '30s, the Cypress Point Club held a tournament in which half the players were members and half were guests, mainly from the East Coast. The East Coast guests came to California and said, "Who can I get a drink from?" That question morphed into "hook-'n-eye," and it became the name of the tournament.

Of course, there was serious violence. Here we are in Chicago. Hello, Al Capone. Hello, St. Valentine's Day Massacre. My hypothesis is that the location of the violence has made a large difference. In the case of Prohibition, the violence took place in the United

States. Everyone could see it and feel it. Everyone could also see that Prohibition was not achieving its presumed objective.

Right now, Mexico bears the burden and Guatemala is being torn up even more than Mexico. Mexico is our next-door neighbor and our third-largest trading partner. The US-Mexico border is the most legally crossed border in the world (lots of commuters). Our culture—as particularly notable in states like California—is heavily influenced by Mexico: the missions, the city names (San Francisco, San Diego, Los Angeles), the streets (I used to live on El Escarpado; El Camino Real seems like an endless street). But somehow we allow ourselves to think that the violence in Mexico is Mexico's problem. The violence is starting to creep north but has not yet reached major proportions or scope.

I suspect that the big difference between drugs and alcohol is that, in the drug case, the violence mostly takes place elsewhere. This is outsourcing, but we should be alarmed, let alone ashamed, that we don't recognize this as our problem.

I have long felt the futility of the present course. Here is a story Pat Moynihan tells in one of his books. At the time, he was a counselor in the Nixon cabinet and I was director of the budget. We were heading to Camp David together, where I was to make a presentation. I'm studying my notes. Pat is in a state of exuberance. Pat says, "Don't you realize? We just had the biggest drug bust in history!" I say, "Congratulations." Pat: "We confiscated fifty tons of cocaine!" I say, "Great work." Pat: "Don't you realize? We've broken the French Connection" (France was the Mexico of that era). He says, "I suppose you think that as long as there is a demand for drugs in this country, there will be a supply." I look at him and say, "Moynihan, there's hope for you."

Gary then asks if there is a better way to reduce drug consumption. He comes to the conclusion recommended by Milton Friedman a long time ago. Gary concludes: "Our study suggests that legalization of drugs combined with an excise tax on consumption would be a far cheaper and more effective way to reduce drug use." Gary's idea is that a tax would raise the price of drugs to warlike levels, so there would be a consistent price discipline of use. The legalization alternative would be vastly different since the revenues would go to government authorities, and the costs in terms of police, imprisonment, violence of drug cartels, and so on, would disappear as, he says, "happened when the prohibition of alcohol ended."

So Gary takes a clear position against the war on drugs. I agree wholeheartedly and have felt this way for some time.

* * *

So, what should we do? Gary talks in his blog about taxation. He would couple legalization with a tax so the price won't fall. So here is my second suggestion as your research assistant, Gary: consider two additional possible ways of influencing the demand curve.

After all, drug dealers want to develop their market, so they get people—particularly young people—hooked. So what is the effect of removing this incentive? You do note that the demand for drugs "is generally quite inelastic," but maybe you can move the demand curve to the left. Additionally, suppose there was a really heavy fact-based advertising campaign along with other efforts, as in the case of cigarettes. Also, create clinics and other centers to provide help to drug users. If you catch the users early, this can be very effective. Could that also move the demand curve to the left?

Now consider another possibility: illegality could be maintained so the drug pushers would still be treated as criminals, and the aura of censure created by illegality, buttressed by an advertising campaign, would still be in place. But decriminalize use and possession of a moderate amount—say, a ten-day supply for personal use. What would happen to the demand curve in these circumstances? Well, I offer you some evidence to go on. That is more or less what has been done in Portugal. The results are not without problems, but the general drift is clear. Decriminalization means that you don't risk jail by going to a treatment center. So what is happening in Portugal? In that country, a consensus emerged that drug abuse was a highly significant problem and that criminalization was exacerbating the problem. So the Portuguese decriminalization was never seen as a concession to the inevitability of drug use but rather as a way to implement "ongoing strategies for prevention, demand reduction, and harm-reduction, as well as maximizing treatment resources and availability for those who seek it" (Greenwald, "Drug Decriminalization," 10).

Special attention needs to be paid to younger age groups. The study I referred to earlier brings out the facts that for two critical groups of youth (thirteen to fifteen years and sixteen to eighteen years), prevalence of use rates have declined for virtually every substance since decriminalization. A chart here shows dramatic reductions for cannabis, cocaine, Ecstasy, amphetamines, heroin, and hallucinatory mushrooms. The study concludes that "in almost every category of drug, and for drug usage overall, the lifetime prevalence rates in the pre-decriminalization era of the 1990s were higher than the post-decriminalization rates" (Greenwald, "Drug Decriminalization," 14).

There is an additional advantage in that taking drugs leads to related diseases, so "the number of newly reported cases of HIV and AIDS among drug addicts has declined substantially every year since 2001" (Greenwald, "Drug Decriminalization," 15).

So, Gary, once again as your research assistant, I ask how you would estimate the impact on the demand curve of the Portuguese approach? Think of the costs avoided, let alone the number of human beings less prone to addiction.

My fourth research issue is a little different. Let me illustrate with a story about the construction business, which I used to be in. If you say to me as a construction guy, "Build me a bridge across the Potomac River," I do my soil tests, order my steel, sink my supports, and construct the bridge. You can drive a truck over it. I can say, "Problem solved. Done with that." If you say to me, "Build a bridge in such a way that there are no lost-time accidents while construction is taking place," and I react by putting up guardrails and other devices and think I've solved the problem, I've lost. The problem is inherently insoluble. Even Gary Becker might have trouble handling it, but he can try. It's about attitudes. So, if I work at it persistently, creatively, professionally, and relentlessly, I just might get the bridge built without lost-time accidents.

The use of drugs has been with mankind for centuries and is no doubt more like the second problem than the first one. We now work at the problem by prosecution, jail time, military intervention, and other efforts to get control of it. This approach, the war on drugs, has failed. The Portuguese effort represents a different approach. Drugs are not condoned, but decriminalization encourages the use of treatment, and that, along with other efforts, represents a different, less costly, and from all the evidence, much more effective way of getting at the problem. So you can't walk away and say, "Problem solved," but you can say, "We are working at the problem in an effective way."

So, Gary, as your research assistant, let me set the problem up for you. We are talking about a process as a way of gaining improvement. Isn't that a description of the way a market works?—a process of continually finding and changing answers, which, with a competition environment, tend to get increasingly attractive.

So, Gary, thanks for your illuminating blogs. To summarize, here are your research assistant's four suggestions for additional work:

1. Look into the degree to which the demand curve can be moved to the left by removing the incentive to develop a market and by effective advertising.
2. We moved much faster to remove Prohibition than we have worked to change the war on drugs. Can we learn anything from this experience? What are the comparative costs, and who bears these costs?
3. Does a change to decriminalization with a framework of illegality offer a promising route, and how would you appraise the Portuguese experience?
4. Finally, we need to find a way to combat the harm to individuals from drug use and the immense costs that accompany present ways of working at the problem by finding a method likely to be more effective.

So, what can take us down the path needed for the big changes advocated by Gary in his blogs?

A. A deep realization in the body politic that we have a large problem, including impending violence that is going to have an impact on many lives.
B. The identification of a sensible program to deal with the problem, such as what is being done in Portugal today.
C. Getting people to discuss the matter openly.
D. I'm afraid some triggering event will be necessary. Unfortunately, the events will probably involve violence.

THE FAILED WAR ON DRUGS

George P. Shultz and Pedro Aspe

Originally published in the New York Times *on January 1, 2018. Pedro Aspe is a former secretary of finance in Mexico.*

The war on drugs in the United States has been a failure that has ruined lives, filled prisons, and cost a fortune. It started during the Nixon administration with the idea that, because drugs are bad for people, they should be difficult to obtain. As a result, it became a war on supply.

As First Lady during the crack epidemic, Nancy Reagan tried to change this approach in the 1980s. But her "Just Say No" campaign to reduce demand received limited support.

Over the objections of the supply-focused bureaucracy, she told a United Nations audience on October 25, 1988: "If we cannot stem the American demand for drugs, then there will be little hope of preventing foreign drug producers from fulfilling that demand. We will not get anywhere if we place a heavier burden of action on foreign governments than on America's own mayors, judges, and legislators. You see, the cocaine cartel does not begin in Medellín, Colombia. It begins in the streets of New York, Miami, Los Angeles, and every American city where crack is bought and sold."[8]

Her warning was prescient but not heeded. Studies show that the United States has among the highest rates of drug use in the world. But even as restricting supply has failed to curb abuse, aggressive policing has led to thousands of young drug users filling American prisons, where they learn how to become real criminals.

The prohibitions on drugs have also created perverse economic incentives that make combating drug producers and distributors extremely difficult. The high black-market price for illegal drugs has generated huge profits for the groups that produce and sell them, income that is invested in buying state-of-the-art weapons, hiring gangs to defend their trade, paying off public officials, and making drugs easily available to children to get them addicted.

Drug gangs, armed with money and guns from the United States, are causing bloody mayhem in Mexico, El Salvador, and other Central American countries. In Mexico alone, drug-related violence has resulted in over 100,000 deaths since 2006. This violence is one of the reasons people leave these countries to come to the United States.

Add it all up and one can see that focusing on supply has done little to curtail drug abuse while causing a host of terrible side effects. What, then, can we do?

First the United States and Mexican governments must acknowledge the failure of this strategy. Only then can we engage in rigorous countrywide education campaigns to persuade people not to use drugs.

The current opioid crisis underlines the importance of curbing demand. This approach, with sufficient resources and the right message, could have a major impact similar to the campaign to reduce tobacco use.

We should also decriminalize the small-scale possession of drugs for personal use, to end the flow of nonviolent drug addicts into the criminal justice system. Several states have taken a step in this direction by decriminalizing possession of certain amounts of marijuana. Mexico's Supreme Court has also declared that individuals should have the right to grow and distribute marijuana for their personal use. At the same time, we should continue to make it illegal to possess large quantities of drugs so that pushers can be prosecuted and some control over supply maintained.

Finally, we must create well-staffed and first-class treatment centers where people are willing to go without fear of being prosecuted and with the confidence that they will receive effective care. The experience of Portugal suggests that younger people who use drugs but are not yet addicted can very often be turned around. Even though it is difficult to get older addicted people off drugs, treatment programs can still offer them helpful services.

With such a complicated problem, we should be willing to experiment with solutions. Which advertising messages are most effective? How can treatment be made effective for different kinds of drugs and different degrees of addiction? We should have the patience to evaluate what works and what doesn't. But we must get started now.

As these efforts progress, profits from the drug trade will diminish greatly even as the dangers of engaging in it will remain high. The result will be a gradual lessening of violence in Mexico and Central American countries.

We have a crisis on our hands—and for the past half century, we have been failing to solve it. But there are alternatives. Both the United States and Mexico need to look beyond the idea that drug abuse is simply a law enforcement problem, solvable through arrests, prosecution, and restrictions on supply. We must together attack it with public health policies and education.

We still have time to persuade our young people not to ruin their lives.

CHAPTER 5

Force and Strength

Force and Strength

Strength makes possible effective diplomacy. The use of force is a means to gain strength, but it only works if it is applied effectively. This is an important distinction, which informed our international relations strategy during the Reagan presidency, from Grenada to the Soviet Union, but it seems to have been forgotten by many today.

The following essays show how this distinction between force and strength has developed in my own thinking. First was an address I delivered while secretary of state in New York in 1984, a year after the war in Grenada and in the midst of a six-day standoff in which passengers were being held on a hijacked airplane on the tarmac of the Tehran airport, some of whom were tortured and killed during negotiations. Less than a year later, another brutal hijacking played out in a Beirut airport, when Lebanese gunmen held hostage American tourists on board TWA flight 847, including traveling members of the US armed services, to demand the release of hundreds of Shia prisoners held by Israel. President Reagan refused on principle to link the two issues and give in to the terrorists' demands; at the same time he resisted calls to retaliate militarily, as it wasn't clear what would be accomplished by doing so, and civilian casualties would have been grave.

Secretary of State George P. Shultz seated with First Lady Nancy Reagan and other cabinet members at a Fourth of July speech by President Ronald Reagan at the Jefferson Memorial, July 1987.
RONALD REAGAN PRESIDENTIAL LIBRARY.

Americans protect our freedoms by maintaining the world's most powerful military. But this overwhelming capability also leaves Americans with the special responsibility to consider the ethics of and goals for using such military force.

In the years since I gave that talk, there has been a tendency to lean heavily on the military to solve all sorts of problems—perhaps because it is the part of the US government that is organized and has the capability to execute. There's always a temptation to say, "Let them do it." Let them solve the drug problem. Or the immigration problem. Let them do this. Let them do that. When I was in office, such projects were resisted by the military, and I think justifiably so—you can't be given every mission. The next essay, then, is an address I gave with that temptation in mind at the Marine Corps University in Quantico, Virginia, in 2017. It is about the interplay between force and strength—and it hinges on the twin ideas of accountability and trust that we explored earlier.

Last is another policy speech from 1984, this one on diplomacy, the twin to force. I was speaking to a group of veterans in Chicago. Secretary of Defense Jim Mattis recently observed that when our country's ability to negotiate foreign policy goals through diplomacy is weakened, "then I need to buy more ammunition." Of course, diplomacy has its limits just as force does. This essay explores that intersection as we think about what ends both those means ultimately serve.

THE ETHICS OF POWER

Address delivered by Secretary of State George P. Shultz at the convocation of Yeshiva University, New York, December 9, 1984. Edited for length.

. . . Today, as we meet, a terrible tragedy is taking place on the other side of the globe. The atrocity of the terrorist hijacking in Tehran continues—a brutal challenge to the international community as well as to the most elementary standards of justice and humanity. One way or another, the law-abiding nations of the world will put an end to terrorism and to this barbarism that threatens the very foundations of civilized life.

Until that day comes, we will all have to wrestle with the dilemmas that confront moral people in an imperfect world. As a nation, we once again face the moral complexity of how we are to defend ourselves and achieve worthy ends in a world where evil finds safe haven and dangers abound.

Today's events make this topic especially relevant, but in fact, it is an old issue. As you know so well, philosophers and sages have grappled with it for centuries, engaging the great questions of human existence: What is the relationship between the individual and his or her God, between the individual and his or her community, and between one's community and the rest of the world? How do we make the difficult moral choices that inevitably confront us as we seek to ensure both justice and survival? The Bible and the commentaries in the Talmud provide many answers; they also leave many questions unanswered, accurately reflecting the predicament of humankind.

As Americans, we all derive from our Judeo-Christian heritage the conviction that our actions should have a moral basis. For the true source of America's strength as a nation has been neither our vast natural resources nor our military prowess. It is, and has always been, our passionate commitment to our ideals.

Unlike most other peoples, Americans are united neither by a common ethnic and cultural origin nor by a common set of religious beliefs. But we are united by a shared commitment to some fundamental principles: tolerance, democracy, equality under the law, and above all, freedom. We have overcome great challenges in our history largely because we have held true to these principles.

The ideals we cherish here at home also guide us in our policies abroad. Being a moral people, we seek to devote our strength to the cause of international peace and justice. Being a powerful nation, we confront inevitably complex choices in how we go about it. With strength comes moral accountability.

Here, too, the intellectual contribution of the Jewish tradition has provided a great resource. The Talmud addresses a fundamental issue that this nation has wrestled with ever since we became a great power with international responsibilities: how to judge when the use of our power is right and when it is wrong. The Talmud upholds the universal law of self-defense, saying, "If one comes to kill you, make haste and kill him first." Clearly, as long as threats exist, law-abiding nations have the right and, indeed, the duty to protect themselves.

The Talmud treats the more complicated issue as well: how and when to use power to defend one's nation before the threat has appeared at the doorstep. Here the Talmud offers no definitive answer. But it is precisely this dilemma that we most often confront and must seek to resolve.

The Need to Combine Strength and Diplomacy

For the world's leading democracy, the task is not only immediate self-preservation but our responsibility as a protector of international peace, on whom many other countries rely for their security.

Americans have always believed deeply in a world in which disputes are settled peacefully—a world of law, international harmony, and human rights. But we have learned through hard experience that such a world cannot be created by goodwill and idealism alone. We have learned that to maintain peace we had to be strong, and more than that, we had to be willing to use our strength. We would not seek confrontation, but we learned the lesson of the 1930s—that appeasement of an aggressor only invites aggression and increases the danger of war. Our determination to be strong has always been accompanied by an active and creative diplomacy and a willingness to solve problems peacefully.

Americans, being a moral people, want our foreign policy to reflect the values we espouse as a nation. But, being a practical people, we also want our foreign policy to be effective. Therefore, we are constantly asking ourselves how to reconcile our morality and our practical sense, how to relate our strength to our purposes—in a word, how to relate power and diplomacy.

How do we preserve peace in a world of nations where the use of military power is an all-too-common feature of life? Clearly, nations must be able to protect themselves when faced with an obvious threat. But what about those gray areas that lie somewhere between all-out war and blissful harmony? How do we protect the peace without being willing to resort to the ultimate sanction of military power against those who seek to destroy the peace?

Americans have sometimes tended to think that power and diplomacy are two distinct alternatives. This reflects a fundamental misunderstanding. The truth is, power and diplomacy must always go together, or we will accomplish very little in this world. Power must always be guided by purpose. At the same time, the hard reality is that diplomacy not backed by strength will always be ineffectual at best, dangerous at worst.

As we look around the world, we can easily see how important it is that power and diplomacy go hand in hand in our foreign policies.

In the Middle East, for instance, the United States is deeply and permanently committed to peace. Our goal has been to encourage negotiation of a peaceful settlement of the Arab-Israeli conflict. At the same time, we have an ironclad commitment to the security of Israel. We believe that Israel must be strong if a lasting peace in the region is to be achieved. The Israeli people must be sure of their own security. They must be sure that their very survival can never be in danger, as has happened all too often in the history of the Jewish people. And everyone in the region must realize that violence, aggression, and extremism cannot succeed, that negotiations are the only route to peace.

In Central America, aggression supported by Nicaragua, Cuba, and the Soviet Union threatens the peace and mocks the yearning of the people for freedom and democracy. Only a steady application of our diplomatic and military strength offers a real hope for peace in Central America and security for the hemisphere. We have sought a dialogue with the Nicaraguan leadership. We have given full support to the Contadora peace efforts. We have provided political and economic support to those in the region who are working for peace and freedom. But we have also provided defense assistance to the region to help establish a shield behind which effective diplomacy can go forward.

I don't know whether any of you have looked closely at the Great Seal of our country, which shows the eagle with its two talons. In one is an olive branch, and the eagle is looking at the olive branch, signifying our desire for peace and reconciliation. But in the other are arrows, symbolizing just this point that I have made, right in the Great Seal of our Republic.

It is as true in our relations with the Soviet Union, and on the issue of arms control, that diplomacy alone will not succeed. We have actively sought negotiation with the Soviet Union to reduce the nuclear arsenals of both sides, but we have also continued to modernize our own forces to ensure our security and that of our friends and allies. No arms control negotiation can succeed in conditions of inequality. Only if the Soviet leaders see the West as determined to modernize its own forces will they see an incentive for agreements setting equal, verifiable, and lower levels of armament.

The Legitimate Use of Power

The need to combine strength and diplomacy in our foreign policies is only one part of the answer. There are agonizing dilemmas inherent in any decision to use our power. But we do not have to look hard to find examples where the use of power has been both moral and necessary.

A week ago, an election was held on the island of Grenada— the first free election held in that country since 1976. If we had not shown the will to use our strength to liberate Grenada, its people would yet be under the tyrant's boot, and freedom would be merely a dream.

Grenada is a tiny country. Although there were some tough actions, as military campaigns go, it was quickly done. But the moral issue it posed was of enormous importance for the United States.

What we did was liberate a country, return it to its own people, and withdraw our forces. We left—even though Grenadians begged us to stay. The American people understood immediately that we had done something good and decent in Grenada—something we could be proud of—even if a few Americans were so mistrustful of their own society that they feared any use of American power. I, for one, am thankful that the president had the courage to do it. Yes, Grenada was a tiny island and relatively easy to save. But what would it have meant for this country—or for our security commitments to other countries—if we were afraid to do even that?

We have to accept the fact that often the moral choices will be much less clearly defined than they were in Grenada. Our morality, however, must not paralyze us. Our morality must give us the strength to act in difficult situations. This is the burden of statesmanship.

And while there may be no clear resolutions to many of the moral dilemmas we will be facing in the future, neither should we be seduced by moral relativism. I think we can tell the difference between the use and abuse of power. The use of power is legitimate

- *not* when it crushes the human spirit and tramples human freedom, but when it can help liberate a people or support the yearning for freedom;
- *not* when it imposes an alien will on an unwilling people, but when its aim is to bring peace or to support peaceful processes, when it prevents others from abusing their power through aggression or oppression; and
- *not* when it is applied unsparingly, without care or concern for innocent life, but when it is applied with the

greatest efforts to avoid unnecessary casualties and with
a conscience troubled by the pain unavoidably inflicted.

Our great challenge is to learn to use our power when it can do
good, when it can further the cause of freedom and enhance international security and stability. When we act in accordance with
our principles and within the realistic limits of our power, we can
succeed. And on such occasions we will be able to count on the
full support of the American people. There is no such thing as
guaranteed public support in advance. Grenada shows that a president who has the courage to lead will win public support if he acts
wisely and effectively. And Vietnam shows that public support can
be frittered away if we do not act wisely and effectively.

Americans will always be reluctant to use force. It is the mark
of our decency. And clearly, the use of force must always be a last
resort, when other means of influence have proven inadequate. But
a great power cannot free itself so easily from the burden of choice.
It must bear responsibility for the consequences of its inaction as
well as for the consequences of its action. In either case, its decision will affect the fate of many other human beings in many parts
of the world.

One need only consider, again, the tragic result of the failure
to use military force to deter Hitler before 1939. If the democracies
had used their power prudently and courageously in the early
stages of that European crisis, they might have avoided the awful
necessity of using far greater force later on, when the crisis had
become an irreversible confrontation. Those responsible for making American foreign policy must be prepared to explain to the
public in clear terms the goals and the requirements of the actions
they advocate. And the men and women who must carry out these
decisions must be given the resources to do their job effectively, so
that we can count on success. If we meet these standards, if we act
with wisdom and prudence, and if we are guided by our nation's
most fundamental principles, we will be a true champion of freedom and bulwark of peace.

If one were looking for a model of how nations should approach
the dilemmas of trying to balance law and justice with self-

preservation, one need look no farther than Israel. It is not that Israel has made no mistakes in its history. In this world, that is too much to ask of any nation. But the people of Israel, in keeping with their tradition, have engaged in open, continual, and enlightened debate over the central question of when it is just and necessary to use power. It is all the more praiseworthy when one considers the great perils to its survival that Israel has faced throughout its history. Its need for strength should be self-evident, yet Israelis never consider the issues of war and peace without debating in terms of right and wrong.

We in America must be no less conscious of the moral responsibility inherent in our role as a great power and as a nation deeply devoted to justice and freedom. We look forward to the day when empire and tyranny no longer cast a shadow over the lives of men and women. We look forward to the day when terrorists, like the hijackers in Tehran, can find not one nation willing to tolerate their existence. But until that day comes, the United States will fulfill the role that history has assigned to us.

The United States must be a tireless sentinel of freedom. We must confront aggression. We must defend what is dear to us. We must keep the flame of liberty burning forever, for all mankind.

Our challenge is to forge policies that keep faith with our principles. We know, as the most powerful free nation on earth, that our burden is great, but so is the opportunity to do good. We must use our power with discretion, but we must not shrink from the challenges posed by those who threaten our ideals, our friends, and our hopes for a better world.

DISCERNING STRENGTH FROM FORCE

Remarks delivered at the Marine Corps University in Quantico, Virginia, on August 4, 2017. Edited for length.

This speech is about the interplay between force and strength. They are not the same, but there's a key interplay. To a very great extent, force is a means to an end, which is strength. So, I'll give a number of examples from my time in the Reagan period, because I know them best, to develop this point.

But let me start first here in Quantico. I came here seventy-five years ago to go to boot camp, and I learned a lot at boot camp and in active duty as a Marine. I remember as though it were yesterday: my drill sergeant hands me my rifle. He says to me, "Take good care of this rifle. This is your best friend. And remember one thing: Never point this rifle at anybody unless you're willing to pull the trigger. No empty threats." Boot camp wisdom. We have seen all too often in recent years the violation of boot camp wisdom, and we've seen how it's cost us. You draw a red line, it's crossed, and you don't do anything. Then no one pays any attention to you; your words don't mean anything. You've got to show you're willing to pull the trigger. And the more people realize that you're willing to pull the trigger, the less likely you are to have to do it. So, that's basic Marine Corps boot camp wisdom.

But there's another side of it, and that is, if you are somebody who does what you say you're going to do and you're a cabinet officer . . . suppose you're negotiating with Congress about something or other or you're in business, or wherever you are, and you're dealing with people. If you say you'll do something, "OK, you'll do this and I'll do that," and you do it, then people trust you and you can deal the next time. But if you don't do it, how am I going to deal with you? You agree to do something and you don't do it, so I can't trust you. So I long ago learned in these things a corollary of the boot camp wisdom: "Trust is the coin of the realm."

So, remember those two things: boot camp wisdom—no empty threats; trust is the coin of the realm.

Now let me give an example of strength. Not long after Ronald Reagan took office, the air traffic controllers went on strike. He said, "They took an oath of office. They violated it. They're out." A clean, principled position. And all over the world, people said, "Is the man crazy? These are the guys that keep the planes flying." But he had eight years of experience as governor of California, and he understood the importance of execution. He had people around who understood that. His secretary of transportation, a guy named Drew Lewis, had been the chief executive of a big transportation company, so he understood the problem, and he had the habit of doing something about problems. And working with the president, they manned the towers with management people, and I think they had some military help, and they had a really aggressive recruiting and training program, and they kept the planes flying. And all over the world, people said, "Hey, watch your step. The guy plays for keeps." So that was an early exhibition of strength, and it helped President Reagan in foreign as well as in domestic problems.

Remember President Reagan's early days. The Vietnam War had been a very discouraging period. Our military daubers were down, and things were dragging. The Carter administration didn't uplift anybody. Ronald Reagan looked over at the Pentagon, and he saw people weren't even wearing their uniforms. We had a big increase in the defense budget, and he said to the people in the Pentagon, "Wear your uniforms! We're proud of you. Be proud of yourselves. Stand up! Salute!" So people started doing that, and the military spirit revived pretty fast.

Then the Cubans invaded a little island state called Grenada. They instituted a really murderous regime. The surrounding island democracies were very upset. We were also upset because a Soviet base was being installed there. They were building a big airport. We thought it was so they could take Soviet bombers, and they could fly to South Africa from there. Furthermore, there was a school on that island, and there were some three hundred Americans going to that school. And we said, "We'll send a boat to take them off." Denied. "We'll send a plane to take them off." Denied. So they were hostages. So this was a huge problem for us.

The island states had a little organization, and they came to us, and they asked for our help in working the problem out. And deliberately, President Reagan said, "We're not going to consult with a lot of people. We want the advantage of surprise." Margaret Thatcher thought she should be consulted because Grenada was part of the Commonwealth, and the Congress also wanted to be consulted. But President Reagan said, "You know, if we have the advantage of surprise, we're going to be able to do the job quickly. If we consult with everybody under the sun, we'll telegraph our punch and it will be much more difficult." So we had an element of surprise. The armed forces—our Marines and others—went in and had a quick military victory. It was very much coordinated between the State Department and the Defense Department, so we knew what our objective was once we succeeded militarily. We wanted to restore the democratic government and get them up and running— help them get going.

We had a quick military victory. It was the first time the United States had used force since Vietnam, so the world all of a sudden realized, "Hey, these guys will pull the trigger." It was quick and clean. We restored the previous democratic government. We said, "Can we help you out?" We fixed the runway and helped their tourist business, did a few other helpful things, and left. So it was a successful case of the use of force with a completely successful diplomatic outcome. The world saw that after Vietnam, yes, we were willing to pull the trigger. That successful use of force gave us strength.

Sometime later, we were having trouble with Iran. Iran was messing with Kuwaiti shipping, so we reflagged the ships to our flag. And while the president of Iran was somewhere making a speech saying that Iran would never even think of putting a mine in the Persian Gulf, our navy was taking pictures of them doing it. We boarded the ship, we took off the sailors, we took off mines for evidence, we sank the ship, we took the sailors to Dubai and said to Iran, "Come and get your sailors and cut it out." There was no loss of life in this operation, but it was a clear display of strength based on the forceful capabilities of the US Navy, so that was a good interplay. We exposed their lie. We let them know we knew what was going on, and there were consequences. So strength was on display.

Let me come to the key issue: the Cold War. This was a big point of tension, and there was a huge argument within the Reagan administration about the Soviet Union. There were many—I think mostly in the Pentagon and the CIA—whose view was: we're here, they're there, that's life; the name of the game is to get along. It was called détente. President Reagan and I thought otherwise. And I had observations when I was secretary of the treasury. One of my jobs was trying to see what I could do about an economic relationship with the Soviet Union, and I saw the weakness of their economy. There wasn't anything they produced that you'd want to buy except their natural resources. I also saw how poor the health care was in the Soviet Union.

I remembered when President Nixon opened our grain markets to them. Teddy Gleason was the longshoremen boss in New York, and he said, "The president of the United States can decide anything he wants, but we ain't loadin' no grain for no Commies!" So that was a problem, so I went down and talked to Teddy, and he agreed to load some grain. And the Soviets, who weren't supposed to know anything about markets, bought a little here, and a little here, and a little here, and before anybody woke up to it, they had this big buy they were going to make, but they had cornered the market. So I went over to Moscow and I had a meeting with Kosygin. He was the number-two guy, and he was in charge of their economic stuff. I said, "Here's what happened," and he said he knew. I said, "You know we can't tolerate that," and he said, "I expect that's true." Then I said, "Well, if you want to have access to our market, we've got to figure out a way to have you compete fairly in the kind of open market that is the wheat market." So we worked out the conceptual basis of what became the Long-Term Grain Agreement: they would tell us what their buy was in the coming season, and we'd agree on some number, and the number would be public so the market would know and their monopsony power was gone. If they wanted to buy more during the season, we could meet again, and if it was okay, we'd announce that. So everything was changed.

Then I got the CIA, with the president's okay, to analyze their farming. With their photography, they could see what was planted and, as the growing season went on, what the crop yields were. And I took this over to our agriculture experts, and they said, "It's appalling the poor yields they have. Our farmers would get double the yields these people get."

And I knew their health care system was a mess. So my view was: we're here, they're there, but they're not stable. They could change. They're going to have to change. And that is what Ronald Reagan's view was. He made a speech to the British Parliament called the Westminster Speech, and startled everybody. He said: They built a wall. Why? We are facing them . . . to prevent them from coming. And their wall is also facing them to prevent their people from coming this way. So what conclusion do you draw from that? And he went on and on.

So we thought things could change, and sometimes little things have a funny impact. I'd had a big trip to China, and I came back to Andrews Air Force Base. It was a Friday. We were lucky to land on a Friday morning because it was snowing. It snowed all day Friday, Friday night, and Saturday. So the Reagans were stuck at the White House. Our phone rings, and Nancy says, "Why don't you come over and have supper with us?" So my wife and I go over, and we sit around, the four of us, having a drink and having supper. And all of a sudden they start asking me about the Chinese leadership. What are they like? Do they have a sense of humor? Can you find their bottom line? And so on. Then they knew I'd dealt with the Soviets and so they started asking about them. President Reagan was doing most of the questioning, but I could see that he and Nancy were very much connected on this. And as I'm sitting there, it's dawning on me: this man has never had a real conversation with a big-time Communist leader, and he's dying to have one.

I had arranged—and it wasn't easy in that atmosphere—to have weekly meetings with Ambassador Dobrynin, the Soviet ambassador in Washington, a very savvy guy. The announced object was, if we see a weed, let's get it out before it grows. There's no point in having problems that we don't need. So I said to the president, "Mr. President, Dobrynin's coming over next Tuesday at five o'clock. Why don't I bring him over here and you talk to him?" He said, "That's a great idea. It will only take ten minutes. All I want to tell him is, if his new leader Andropov [who had just succeeded Brezhnev] is interested in a constructive conversation, I'm ready." That was thunderbolt news. But as a result of this conversation, I knew where his gut was, and most other people didn't.

So I bring him over. We're there for at least an hour and a half and talk about everything under the sun. I'm sure Dobrynin must have been amazed at the president's knowledge and comfort in talking about rather complicated arms control–type things. But he spent a lot of his time talking about Soviet Jewry and their mishandling of them, and it wasn't just a generalization; he had names, he had incidents to talk about, so it was rather impressive. And then you may remember, during the Carter administration, a group of seven or eight Pentecostals rushed into our embassy, and you couldn't expel them because they would probably be killed, but it was kind of an uncomfortable situation, and President Reagan kept saying, "It's like a big neon sign in Moscow: we don't treat people right; we don't let them worship the way they want; we don't let them emigrate. We ought to do something about it." He kept saying all the time, "All I want is for something to happen. I won't say a word. I just want something to happen."

So Dobrynin and I rode back to the State Department and talked about it, and we said, "Let's make that our special project." So we exchanged papers back and forth. I'm presuming his go back to Moscow. And finally I got one that I thought was pretty good, and I took it over to the president. I said, "Mr. President, if you call in your lawyer, he'll tell you that you can drive a truck through the holes in this memo, but I have to believe, with all the background of this, that if we get them out of the embassy, they'll be allowed to go home and eventually emigrate." So we thought about it and talked about it. We rolled the dice and got them to leave the embassy, and they were allowed to go home. A few months later, they were not only allowed to emigrate; all their families—about fifty or sixty people—were allowed to leave. It was a huge event. Ronald Reagan said nothing. I said to him, "The deal is, Mr. President, we'll let them free if you don't talk," and he didn't. I thought to myself, "You know, that little incident had some bigger implications than you might think." Nobody knew what had happened, but I knew. He saw that you could make a deal with these people and they would carry it out, and they saw the same thing. They knew how tempting it is for an American politician to say, "Look what I did," but he didn't do it. So we had that little incident.

But then the big deal is the Cold War. The Soviets had deployed something called intermediate-range nuclear weapons—INF weapons—and their diplomatic ploy was that these weapons could hit European targets, hit Japan, hit China, but they couldn't hit us. And their diplomacy was based on one theme: would we use our intercontinental missiles, risking retaliation from them with their intercontinental missiles? So, their effort was to divide us from our allies. So we made a deal in NATO that we would have a negotiation with them, and if we couldn't get a satisfactory conclusion, we would deploy our own INF weapons in Europe. On the intermediate range missiles, we had none deployed; they had some fifteen hundred. Our position was zero on both sides, and people said, "What a ridiculous position." We said, "Well, that's what we want, so that's our position." So we start this negotiation. President Reagan was very aware that he was not just having a negotiation with the Soviet Union; he was also engaging with the European public, because if you're going to deploy a nuclear weapon somewhere, that's a target, and that makes you uneasy, so we had to have that constantly on our minds.

As we worked through our negotiating position, we changed it from time to time. We had lots of consultation in an effort to be sure the Europeans understood we were bargaining in good faith. Then we broke another of the shibboleths of the Cold War, having broken with détente, and that was linkage. If something happened in this area, everything else stopped. So when they went into Afghanistan, President Carter cut off all relations. Nothing: athletes can't go to the Olympics; no contacts at all. That was a frozen situation and that's what we inherited.

While this negotiation was going on, the Soviets shot down a Korean airliner. We led the charge in condemning that action. But we broke with the concept of linkage. I went ahead with a scheduled meeting with Gromyko, and at one point he got up to leave and I said, "Go ahead and leave," and he sat back down. But he got so angry he went out to the big meeting and said, "If somebody flies an airliner across our territory again, we'll shoot it down again," so he lost the argument internationally because he got so aggravated.

At any rate, we sent our negotiators back to Geneva, and that was by way of saying to the Europeans, "This effort is in good faith. We're not just sitting there." The end of 1983 comes along, and we're still working. But it's clear that negotiations are going nowhere. So we deployed cruise missiles in Britain; Margaret Thatcher helped us with that. We deployed cruise missiles in Italy, and Andreotti helped us with that. Cruise missiles, of course, are one thing. But the big deal was the deployment of ballistic missiles in Germany. They were called Pershings. This was a giant effort. The Soviets thought the Pershings could reach Moscow, so the idea of Germany being able to exterminate Moscow was nerve-racking. So the Soviets pulled out of negotiations and fanned war talk. It was really tense going. But the alliance held together. The president of France went to the Bundestag and talked. We were very active. All the other allies pitched in to support Germany. We deployed the missiles. I thought it was Helmut Kohl's finest hour as chancellor of Germany.

So the Soviets, as I said, walked out of negotiations. They fanned war talk. It was tough going, but we deployed. That was a statement of strength.

Over time, gradually things died down, and by August of the following year, 1984, I was able to go to the president and say, "Mr. President, at four different European capitals, a Soviet diplomat has come up to one of ours and said virtually the same thing, which we think boils down to: if Foreign Minister Gromyko is invited to Washington when he comes to the General Assembly in September, he'll accept. In other words, the Soviets blinked. I said,

"Maybe you want to think this over because when they invaded Afghanistan, President Carter ended these meetings, which were traditional meetings, and they're still there." He said, "I don't have to think it over. Let's get him here."

So he came. It was a giant event. There was an interesting little sidebar. Nancy Reagan was a pal of mine. At White House dinners, she always fixed me up with a Hollywood starlet as my dinner partner, so I got to dance with Ginger Rogers. There's a picture of us dancing. I sent it to Ginger, and she wrote on it, "Dear George, What fun. For the first few minutes, I thought I was dancing with Fred. Let's do it again! Love, Ginger."

So I went to Nancy and said, "Nancy, what's going to happen is Gromyko is going to come to the Oval Office; we'll have probably a reasonably long meeting, and the president may want to have a little side one-on-one. Then we'll all walk down the colonnade to the mansion. That's your home. There'll be some stand-around time and then we'll have a working lunch. So it would be a nice gesture of hospitality if you were there for the stand-around. After all, it's your home and you're the hostess. She said okay. So we walked down the colonnade, and Gromyko, who's a smart diplomat, sees Nancy and knows she's influential, so he makes a beeline to her. After a while, he says to her, "Does your husband want peace?" Nancy could bristle. She said, "Of course my husband wants peace!" Then he says, "Well then, every night before he goes to sleep, whisper in his ear, 'Peace.'" He was a little taller than she was, so she put her hands on his shoulders and pulled him down so he had to bend his knees. She said, "I'll whisper it in *your* ear, 'Peace.'" I said to her, "Nancy, you just won the Cold War."

At any rate, after that, President Reagan won the election in a landslide. We even got a note from the Soviet general secretary, Chernenko. He'd read Ronald Reagan's speeches in which he'd talked about the fact that he thought nuclear weapons were immoral and we should get rid of them. Chernenko's message was, we've been reading your speeches and we think maybe you're right, and we could discuss that.

Then in January, I went over to Geneva and met with Gromyko, and we restarted the arms negotiations, so we were back on track.

All of this happened before Gorbachev. Then Gorbachev comes, and Gromyko and I have a meeting, and we set the dates for a meeting with President Reagan and Gorbachev in Geneva. Then I'm sitting next to Gromyko at dinner. (He spoke English, of course.) He's telling me about Gorbachev's program of trying to get Russians to stop drinking so much vodka, so they were making it hard to get vodka. I said to him, "You'd better be careful about that. We tried it in our country and it didn't work too well." I said, "You also have to worry about street humor." He said, "What do you mean, street humor?" I said, "Well, there's a story going around in Moscow about these two guys standing in line at the vodka store. Half an hour goes by, an hour goes by, and they're inching up in the line. One of them says, 'I'm sick of this. I'm going over to the Kremlin to shoot Gorbachev,' and he leaves. About half an hour later, he comes back. His buddy has moved up in line a little. And his buddy says, 'Well, did you shoot him?' He says, 'Hell, no. The line up there is a lot longer than this one.'" Gromyko didn't think that was funny.

The point of this story is that the deployment of the Pershing missiles was the turning point in the Cold War. It was an exhibition of extraordinary strength. Not a shot was fired. It was a weapon, but there was no force in the sense of active shooting. But it was a tremendous act of strength. Then, of course, things progressed, and we did have basically an end to the Cold War.

All of these things boil down to the importance of force and the importance of using it effectively. If it's used ineffectively, it can deprive you of strength. And if you ignore boot camp wisdom, you're going to undermine your strength tremendously.

POWER AND DIPLOMACY

Address delivered by Secretary of State George P. Shultz to the Veterans of Foreign Wars, Chicago, August 20, 1984. Edited for length.

. . . If history has taught us anything, it is that effective diplomacy depends on strength. Dwight Eisenhower—in whose name you are honoring me tonight—understood it well. "Military power," he once told the Congress, "serves the cause of peace by holding up a shield behind which the patient, constructive work of peace can go on."

It has been almost forty years since the end of the Second World War, a war in which many of you fought. You fought—and many Americans died—not only to defend our nation but to free the world from a brutal tyranny. The American people hoped that with victory would come a better world in which peace and prosperity would reign and war would be a thing of the past. But we learned soon after the war that there are no final victories: the struggle between freedom and tyranny goes on; the United States, as the leader of the democracies, cannot evade its continuing responsibility to promote freedom and prosperity and to defend what we hold dear.

The Purpose of Negotiations

Dwight Eisenhower, as a great military leader and a great president, knew that America's strength was moral as well as military and economic. Our power was the servant of our positive goals, our values, and ideals. We Americans have always deeply believed in a world in which disputes were settled peacefully—a world of law, international harmony, and human rights. But we have learned through hard experience, in World War II and after, that such a world cannot be created by goodwill and idealism alone. Since 1945, every president, Democratic or Republican, has understood that to maintain the peace we had to be strong, and more than that, we had to be willing to use our strength. We would not seek confrontation, but we would never appease or shrink from the challenge posed by threats of aggression. And this determination was always accompanied by an active and creative diplomacy and a willingness to solve problems peacefully.

President Kennedy defined the two goals of this solidly bipartisan approach in his inaugural address: "Let us never negotiate out of fear," he said, "but let us never fear to negotiate."

In the years that followed, however, the consensus behind this balanced approach began to show signs of strain. For whatever reason, Vietnam created doubts in the minds of some that peace and military strength were compatible. The lessons so clearly understood by President Eisenhower, it seemed, were being forgotten. And today, even though we have overcome the trauma of Vietnam, one gets the sense that some still believe that power and diplomacy are alternatives. From one side, we hear that negotiations alone are the answer. If we will only talk (the argument runs), we can have peace. If we will only talk, our differences will easily be resolved. It is as if negotiations were an end in themselves, as if the goal of American foreign policy were not primarily to protect the peace, or defend our values, or our people, or our allies, but to negotiate for its own sake. From another side, though the chorus is considerably smaller, we hear that we should never negotiate, never compromise with our adversaries, because the risks are too great and the differences irreconcilable.

Both views are as wrong today as they would have been four decades ago. Negotiations are not the goal of American foreign policy; they are a means of attaining that goal. In fact, they are an essential means. But we know, as surely as we know anything, that negotiations and diplomacy not backed by strength are ineffectual at best, dangerous at worst.

As your secretary of state, I can tell you from experience that no diplomacy can succeed in an environment of fear or from a position of weakness. No negotiation can succeed when one side believes that it pays no price for intransigence and the other side believes that it has to make dangerous concessions to reach agreement. This is true whether we are talking about Vietnam or Lebanon or Central America; it is true in arms control and in our relations with the

Soviet Union. Americans have only to remember what we understood so well four decades ago: neither strength nor negotiations are ends in themselves. They must go hand in hand.

And I can also tell you that any strategy, to be effective, must be sustainable over the long haul. It cannot be sustained if our policies vacillate wildly in response to events beyond our control. Americans are by nature a people of action, and we are sometimes impatient with a world that progresses slowly. When Americans act, we want to see clear and quick results. And the pattern of the recent past has been one of excessive expectations, which, when unfulfilled, have led to equally excessive reversals in policy. This inconsistency has hindered the achievement of American goals.

We do not negotiate with our adversaries because we think they are perfectible. Nor do we negotiate just to please this or that domestic constituency. We negotiate because it is in our country's interest to do so, and we reach agreements when we perceive that both we and our adversaries can gain from a negotiated solution. To negotiate on those terms is to deal with the world as it is, without illusions.

We know that negotiations with the Soviet Union, for instance, are not a panacea. Yet we know that equitable and verifiable agreements can make a significant contribution to stability in the nuclear age or to the resolution of conflicts that might otherwise escalate and threaten to overwhelm us. To negotiate to these ends is the only prudent and responsible course. It serves American interests.

If our proposals are rejected and unreciprocated—as they have been of late—we must show staying power. Sometimes it seems as if the Soviets won't take yes for an answer. At the same time, we should not seek agreement for the sake of agreement or allow occasional successes to give rise to unwarranted euphoria. Our interests require that we stay on course despite the periodic disappointments and setbacks that we are bound to encounter in dealing with such a ruthless competitor. Unfortunately, outrageous incidents, such as the Korean airliner attack or the persecution of Andrei Sakharov, are what we must expect. However shocking, they do not come as surprises that require us to reassess and change our basic strategy, including our strategy of willingness to negotiate.

Patience is a virtue in foreign affairs as much as in our personal lives. If we keep our eye on our strategic objectives, if we negotiate without illusions, if we use our strength effectively, we will see progress. The truth is, we advance our interests less by the big, obvious successes, by summits, by decisive battles, by glamorous international agreements, than we do by our permanent engagement and by the steady application of sound policies.

The Tide of Freedom

Let's look at Central America. It is no coincidence that when America has shown consistency and commitment in Central America, progress in that region has been equally consistent. We all know what the problem is in Central America: Nicaragua's push toward militarism and totalitarianism. We have seen increased repression, persecution of the church, a massive influx of Soviet arms, and continued aggression against Nicaragua's neighbors. Today we hear of Nicaraguan elections promised for November. The notion of democracy is so powerful that even dedicated Marxist-Leninists feel they have to show that they are holding elections. Feeling the pull of the tide of true democracy that is running now in Central and South America, they seek to represent their elections as meaningful. But they are not succeeding. The failures of the Nicaraguan regime have generated a determined internal opposition—the true Sandinistas. Because of the regime's efforts to suppress that internal opposition, the elections promised for November now look more and more like sham elections on the Soviet model.

America has responded with patience and consistent policies based on strength and diplomacy. We have sought a dialogue with the Nicaraguan leadership. We have given our full support to the Contadora peace efforts. But we have also maintained an American military presence in the region to serve as the shield, in President Eisenhower's words, behind which effective diplomacy can go forward. We have provided economic, political, and military support for the free elected government of El Salvador.

And we admire the dedication of the Nicaraguan freedom fighters, who want only to bring democracy to their people. All these forces help provide the strength and the purpose essential if a solution is to be found that ends the fear and agony in Central America and opens a promising future of peace, freedom, and prosperity.

Our policies are working. Gradually, but inevitably, Communist aggression is losing the contest. Hope is being created for the people of Central America. Success will not come overnight, and we cannot let our policies vacillate in response to emotions or political passions at home. Only a steady, purposeful application of our diplomatic and military strength offers real hope for peace in Central America and security for the hemisphere.

We can see similar signs of progress throughout the world. While there are always obstacles and occasional setbacks, the broader picture is a hopeful one. The day-to-day events of foreign policy are like waves rolling up against the shore. Some break in one direction; some break in the other. But what is more important than the path of a single wave is the flow of the tide beneath it. Is the tide rising or is it falling? Is the course of history on the side of peace, freedom, and democracy? Or is America standing on weak ground against inevitable and ineluctable forces?

The tide of history is with us. The values that Americans cherish—democratic freedom, peace, and the hope of prosperity—are taking root all around the world. Look again at Latin America. Despite grave economic problems and Communist efforts to exploit them, almost every nation in that region is either democratic or on the path toward democracy. Never before have more people in our hemisphere had such hope of tasting the fruits of true freedom. This gradual movement does not receive the attention of the media as much as the sporadic guerrilla offensive, but it is there. It is undeniable. The tide in Latin America is the tide of freedom.

Restoration of Confidence

A month ago, I visited our friends and allies in Southeast Asia. Our relations with those nations have never been stronger, in large part because the values we Americans cherish are also flourishing in those faraway lands. Japan, Korea, Australia, and New Zealand are valued allies and vibrant societies; the free Southeast Asian nations, ASEAN [Association of South East Asian Nations], are embarked on the same journey toward freedom and democracy; their economic success symbolizes how far they have come. The US-China relationship is maturing and broadening as we identify and develop common interests. Our deepening friendship with these nations gets few headlines, but it marks the fact that in the decade since Vietnam, the United States has restored its position and its relations in Asia. And, increasingly, the real lesson of Vietnam is clear. The world now condemns Vietnam's aggression in Kampuchea. The steady outflow of refugees from areas dominated by Hanoi is showing the Vietnamese Communists for what some of us always knew they were.

In Europe, we have faced periodic crises, moments of apparent disunity, and times when Soviet intimidation has jostled relations with our oldest and closest friends. The Soviets once thought they could split the NATO alliance by pointing SS-20 nuclear missiles at the free peoples of Western Europe. But these tests of the alliance's strength have served only to prove one thing: that the solidarity of democratic nations endures, that the transatlantic bonds are strong and secure. Our shared moral values and political principles have made NATO the keeper of the peace for thirty-five years and will continue to do so into the next century and beyond.

Indeed, if there is weakness in Europe, it is within the Soviet empire. The yearning for democracy and freedom in the countries of Eastern Europe is a powerful and growing force. We have seen it in recent years among the brave people of Poland, as we saw it in Czechoslovakia in 1968, in Hungary in 1956, and in East Germany in 1953. We will never accept the idea of a divided Europe. Time is not on the side of imperial domination. We may not see freedom in Eastern Europe in our lifetime. Our children may not see it in theirs. But someday it will happen. The world's future is a future of freedom.

Make no mistake. History will do us no special favors. A better future depends on our will, our leadership, our willingness to act decisively in moments of crisis, and our ability to be constant and steadfast in moments of calm. We must be ready to engage ourselves where necessary throughout the world. We must be ready to use our diplomatic skills and our military strength in defense of our values and our interests.

There was a time, a decade or so ago, when some Americans may have doubted that their great nation could continue to be a force for good in the world. But today Americans no longer doubt America's ability to play its proper role. In the past four years, this nation has taken the essential steps to restore its leadership of the free world. We have restored the strategic balance. We have restored the strength and thrust of our dynamic economy. We have restored our will and self-confidence. We have restored national pride and respect for the men and women who serve in our armed forces. And we have restored the confidence of our friends and allies around the world that America can be trusted to confront challenges, not wish them away.

I don't mean to suggest that the path ahead of us is easy. But in the face of the forces of tyranny, we draw inspiration from the basic goodness of America, and our pride in our country gives us strength to lead abroad.

No one understands or feels that pride more deeply than you, who have defended this great nation in times of national peril. You knew what you were fighting against and what you were fighting for. And you knew what kind of people you were defending—a people devoted to freedom and justice, a brave people willing to sacrifice for what they believe. And it is your sacrifices that have made peace possible. You laid the foundation for the kind of world we all seek. Let us never forget that as we look toward the future.

Americans must never be timid, or ashamed, or guilt-ridden, or weak. We are proud and strong—and confident. We will use our power and our diplomacy in the service of peace and our ideals. We have our work cut out for us. But we feel truly that the future is bright.

CHAPTER 6

Practicing Theories
of Governance

CHAPTER 6

Practicing Theories
of Governance

Governance is always hard, but these days it is even more difficult because of the flood of information that inundates all of us, whether in government or in the private sector. I've included two speeches here that relate to what I'll call the operational aspects of governance.

The first is about understanding what different parts of the government can and cannot do well. The idea that cities or counties or states have their ears closer to ground and so can be more nimble in responding to the concerns of a diverse electorate is not new. The founding fathers early on recognized the differences among the states and their interests. James Madison, in the Federalist Papers, took on a contemporary criticism of democratic governance—its tendency toward "mob rule," and therefore instability—by arguing that governance in the country should actually encourage the expression of such diversity of interests and opinion as a form of competition and even self-regulation. In Federalist No. 10 he writes:

> As long as the reason of man continues fallible, and he is at liberty to exercise it, different opinions will be formed. As long as the connection subsists between his reason

and his self-love, his opinions and his passions will have a reciprocal influence on each other; and the former will be objects to which the latter will attach themselves. . . . The diversity in the faculties of men, from which the rights of property originate, is not less an insuperable obstacle to a uniformity of interests. *The protection of these faculties is the first object of government.* [Emphasis added]

Madison argued that cultivating as many diverse interests as possible within an expanding union would create a political and social system less likely to be dominated by any single faction. He even thought it could stop the spread of extremism. Were the state to limit any one interest, however, it risked putting an unbalanced weapon in the hands of another. Madison's words were echoed by Thomas Jefferson, who late in life suggested, in reference to his championing of religious plurality in Virginia, "Divided we stand, united we fall."[9]

Applying that insight, the authors of our Constitution provided for a balance of power in governmental institutions in Washington, DC, and argued that most issues, leaving aside defense and foreign policy, should be left to the states and localities. If decisions were different from each other, so be it. We can have a Chinatown in San Francisco. Maybe you'll find something different in New Orleans. Both are fine.

Of course, it's hard to easily laud the federalist system's effective governance of diversity if we consider the African American experience. Left to their own, the states did not handle that well, and we ultimately amended the Constitution three times to help this and other groups of Americans, expanding federal power in the process.

But the federal government has tended over time to expand its grasp over the localities in far less deserving areas as well. I had this troubling trend in mind when I delivered this 1970 speech, "The New Federalism," while secretary of labor in the Nixon administration.

Perhaps surprisingly, the idea of states and cities doing things their own way has now reemerged with a new group of supporters, given differences in this country over policies such as drug control, immigration, and the environment. And I tend to support that expression of diversity—a new sort of federalism. Let's try to sort out from scratch what belongs in our nation's capital and what belongs in states and local governmental institutions and what belongs to individual choice. After all, the government doesn't tell us where to go to church or where to buy our groceries or where to send our children to school. Some people today have more choice than others, and we should work hard to maximize choice all around.

Incidentally, we can see how the question of governing over diversity has played out in other countries where the United States has been involved, too. I've never been in Afghanistan, but I once went to the Khyber Pass on the Pakistan border. From there, you can see Afghanistan as a mountainous country with lots of natural divisions. Historically, it was a diverse country, run by a network of warlords but in a decentralized way. I've always wondered if we didn't make a mistake, after our brilliant military success working with the Northern Alliance post-9/11, in then letting our mission change to creating an Afghanistan that's democratically governed from Kabul, with a centralized army that keeps the peace.

In my opinion, which is perhaps not widely shared, that's not Afghanistan. We have been there all these years, and we are not succeeding. It seems to me that today we could still say, "Let's respect the decentralized nature of the country and work with the various decentralized elements to create security where we can within their territories," warlords or not. It's our goal to stabilize the country. It's not our goal to try to upend history and revolutionize everything from Kabul. What we think of as corruption, for example, is what they may think of as just the way of doing things: the culture clash is very deep. It's important to get the concept right.

Returning to an earlier theme from this book, as an individual in society, you have more confidence in people who are accountable. They tell you what they intend to do and then go about doing it—and if they fail, you can do something about it. At the same time, you also want the people governing you to be trustworthy. Think of this in your personal life: you can deal effectively with people you trust, but if you don't trust someone, that person is difficult to deal with. Accountability and trust are key issues in appraising the quality of governance. Together these two points argue for having as much governance as possible done near where you are, by people you know. And the same goes for administration: even in cases where policies must be set on a broad basis, administration of those policies is often, if not always, most effectively carried out by the people close to those affected.

The second speech I have included in this chapter gets to the part of governance where even those who are supposed to be working together to deliver a given administration's policy don't agree. You could say that this one even ended up in my resigning as secretary of treasury in the Nixon administration—though that wasn't my intent at the time. While you can't nitpick so much that you threaten to resign every time things don't go your way, if something is really important and it's in your area, then you have to think it over.

In the early 1970s, when I was director of the Office of Management and Budget for a short period following my stint as secretary of labor, I could see that a certain faction within the administration favored the institution of broad economic wage and price controls as a way to control the high inflation of the time. And I thought that would be a catastrophe.

So, in 1971 I made a speech to the Economic Club of Chicago titled "Steady as You Go," arguing that we already had the federal budget under control, and with the right kind of monetary policy, inflation would eventually come under control too. The cycle of wage negotiations between labor and management was thought to play a role in inflation pressures, so I drew on my understanding of that realm from my previous job in the Department of Labor to make that case.

For a while the proponents were held at bay, but ultimately I lost the argument, and the Nixon administration ended up putting a wage and price control system into place.

I had opposed it in part because the free market system is, at its core, a system of accountability. If you let it work, the accountability is relentless in punishing bad performances and rewarding good ones. If you intervene in this accountability system, though, you inevitably change it and can easily wind up moving responsibility to the intervener, usually the government. And that's what happened.

At first, the president's controls program wasn't my responsibility. But then I became secretary of the treasury, and with that, the newly created Cost of Living Council, which administered the controls, would be reporting to me. So, we tried to ease off the system, but as Milton Friedman had warned earlier, controlling prices despite background inflationary pressure meant that we had caught a tiger by its tail. Market prices exploded as soon as we relaxed them, and President Nixon reacted very strongly, deciding to reimpose wage and price controls. So I said to him, "Mr. President, I recognize this is your call, but I don't agree with it. I think it's a very bad call for the economy—which now reports to me. So you've got to get yourself a new secretary of the treasury." I resigned. The president accepted, but I actually ended up staying in that job at his request for nearly another year to continue managing US-Soviet and other global economic relationships, which turned out to be helpful background given later responsibilities.

More broadly, this problem of how individual members of an administration do their jobs—how their responsibilities are structured and how they are hired in the first place—has become a bigger problem over time. And it contributes to our current crisis in governance. In our constitutional form of government, an elected president is able to appoint the leadership—secretary, undersecretary, assistant secretaries, and so on—of the departments and agencies that have been created by acts of Congress and which are otherwise staffed by a set of permanent government employees. These leaders are appointed by the president, subject to confirmation by the Senate, and they are responsible for what goes on. They can be called to testify to Congress, under oath. That's the accountable line management of the US government, and it works.

In recent years, though, two things have happened that break down this system. One is that it's hard to get the best people—who often have other opportunities in the private sector—through the tortuous confirmation process. Somebody is asked and says, "Yes, I'll serve." Before you know it, they are disconnected from whatever they're already doing, filling out endless forms—financial information and everything else too, all subject to criminal penalties. Then they wait around to get a hearing, and when it comes, it's not very elevating. Committee members ask questions for cameras; they're not really interested in the answers. Eventually they are voted out of committee, but maybe a senator has some special thing that he or she wants, so they create a hold to prevent a floor vote. It has nothing to do with the appointee, who is just a device. When it takes a year before finally taking office, it's not surprising that people say, "My gosh, that's not a very good deal." Instead, it would be better to get back to the assumption that honorable people want to serve honorably, and if you get a bad apple, you throw him out. You find it out pretty fast.

This problem is confounded by the fact that, in part since it's so hard to get through that formal confirmation process, the White House ends up hiring its own duplicate executive staff instead. They don't have to stand for confirmation, are not callable before Congress, and usually plead executive privilege. They are in effect making policy, but they are unaccountable. And of course that makes it even more difficult to get people willing to serve in the agencies, because once they get in the job, the cabinet members find out they are reporting to a White House staffer rather than the president.

When agency leaders are the ones involved in developing policy, it is executed better because those who helped develop it are the ones administering it. Furthermore, they benefit from the collective experience and expertise of the agency's permanent staff—and they know a lot. So while it seems obscure, fixing these sorts of operational issues lets you attract higher-quality people and get better policy making—and you'll see better execution too. The name of the game is always people.

THE NEW FEDERALISM

Address delivered at the Conrad Hilton Hotel, in Chicago, to the annual management conference of the University of Chicago Graduate School of Business, March 19, 1970.

I don't think the Nixon administration is being well enough criticized.

I didn't say we weren't being criticized enough. I said not *well* enough. Here is what I mean:

In domestic as well as foreign affairs, the president is pursuing a strategy. You may not agree with his strategy, but I think you owe it to yourselves to come to grips with that strategy, to try to understand this administration's philosophy, so you can criticize it fairly and constructively.

One of the clichés of this administration is a phrase taken from professional football: "game plan." Whenever I make a proposal, whenever we come up with a new tactic, we have to show how it fits in the overall game plan.

Today, I would like to go beyond the confines of being a spokesman in the field of labor to try to explain what our administration's game plan is. There are some who will call it madness, but even they will have to admit there is some method in it.

Let me begin by suggesting what our method is *not*. We are not professional zigzaggers. We are not trying to sell liberal principles with conservative rhetoric, or vice versa. We are not trying to heal the nation's differences by "splitting the difference."

Our preference for a theoretical underpinning shows in many ways. At a Washington Redskins football game last season, there was a blatantly bad call by the referee on pass interference. Edward Bennett Williams, owner of the team, yelled, "Bad call!" Former Chief Justice Warren, sitting next to him, said in a dignified way, "Poor judgment." And Henry Kissinger rose to his feet, shook his fist at the referee, and shouted, "On what theory?"

* * *

We ask ourselves, "On what theory?" all the time. The theory, or political philosophy, that has emerged after one year has been called the New Federalism. I submit to you that it is more than a catch phrase; it is a new approach, one that has evolved from the national experience, one deserving careful analysis by thoughtful men.

To grasp the new approach, you have to cast out one of the basic measurements of political ideology—the idea of liberal versus conservative, the old political spectrum of left and right. It will be a wrench to set aside this familiar caliper, but it does not measure what is going on in government today.

That is because, in the past decade, liberals and conservatives found themselves using the same language in describing their common complaints.

Liberals were complaining that government was becoming unresponsive—that there was a greater need for local and citizen involvement. This sounded like the old conservative demand for decentralization.

Conservatives, on the other hand, were saying that our welfare system and our educational establishment were in need of fundamental reform, to correct the unfairness built in over three decades of trying to cure social ills. Liberals found little to argue about in that.

It was as if the nation had gone through a gigantic halftime, and the old opponents had switched sides, each now marching toward the other's former goal.

But the change is deeper than that. The change centered on a unique area of agreement. As labor secretary, it is my job to discover areas of agreement in what appear to be positions of great dispute, and I can certainly see one here.

Liberals and conservatives agree on the need for a new fairness in American life. And hopefully, through this new sense of fairness we can achieve greater efficiency in the administration of domestic affairs.

Liberals and conservatives agree on the need for a selective decentralization of government.

Liberals and conservatives agree on a reform of our institutions that makes the setting of national standards a national affair and makes the detailed administration of government programs a very local affair.

The New Federalism broadens and deepens these areas of agreement. In essence, the New Federalism calls upon us to act as one nation in setting the standards of fairness, and then to act as congeries of communities in carrying out those standards. We are nationalizing equity as we localize control, while retaining a continued federal stewardship to ensure that national standards are attained.

* * *

The best way to explain any theory is to cite examples. And the examples are there, in the field of labor and in many others.

Take welfare. A national sense of fairness says that a man who is working ought to make more than a man who is not working. A national common sense says that a working man who makes less than a man on welfare across the street will be inclined to *stop* working.

To introduce that element of fairness in our family assistance proposal, we aim to assist the working poor in a way that will always make it profitable to work.

But to permit diversity, to encourage localities and states to make their own decisions on the degree to which they want to help the less fortunate, we provide an income floor but no ceiling. It is up to the states and cities to administer large portions of this program consistent with national goals and to decide for themselves how much more they are able to do.

Thus, we have a *national minimum* on family assistance—as the president puts it, "no child is worth more in one state than in another," as far as the federal government is concerned. At the same time, we have *local participation* in administration and local say-so on what more should be done. National fairness, local diversity.

* * *

Take manpower training, really a classic example of this New Federalism. On the national level, we recognize the need for training people for new and better jobs, and the need to fund this activity. But most labor markets are local in scope: this is where the action is, and this is where the best judgment concerning the use of resources should be. The basic way we have proposed to handle this situation is to provide incentives for state and local government and private sponsors to get into the act, while providing more money and more local control in specific stages, as localities develop the means to put these programs into action. Again, national fairness, local assumption of control.

Another example in the labor area: safety standards. Two million workers a year are injured on the job. On the federal level, the president's proposal would set up a national Occupational Safety and Health Board; its standards are to be adapted and administered by the states, as they demonstrate their capacity to take over. The enforcement of safety standards is local, with national monitors. The federal government pays 90 percent of the state's planning costs, then shares the administrative costs on a fifty-fifty basis. Again, national standards, local administration and enforcement, a reserve federal "clout."

Attaining our national goal of equal opportunity in employment is another example of the New Federalism. Where federal funds are used, affirmative action can be used to eliminate discrimination in employment on the part of management or labor. In our Philadelphia Plan, we put this into practical action in the construction industry for the first time—and not without considerable controversy. But there is no necessity for the mechanical application of federal standards if local people can work out a strong agreement among themselves. In this case, as in so many others, there is no solution like a hometown solution—provided it works toward our national goal.

* * *

I could cite a dozen other examples of this New Federalist approach: in our environmental program, which sets antipollution standards and provides for local enforcement and a sharing of the financing of treatment facilities; in tax policy, which removes seven million poor from the tax rolls and provides a greater incentive to start working; in our computerized job bank, which looks toward a national information system with local and regional participation and control.

In case after case, the pattern is clear: a concern for fairness as a nation, a concern for diversity as a people, a recognition of federal stewardship.

But while it is a clear pattern, it is not a simple one. You cannot label this "decentralization"—because the establishment of so many national standards, in *so* many fields, is a form of centralization. But this is done in a way that does not dehumanize and depersonalize government, resulting in alienated people and ineffective bureaucracy. It is done in a way that decentralizes administration and encourages local participation, bringing about the best of both worlds—fairness and citizen involvement. At least, that is what we are hoping to do.

By taking this tack, we hope to reinstill in the American people their faith in the responsiveness of their government to what they consider to be fair.

By following this method we call the New Federalism, we hope to reinstill self-reliance on the part of individuals and strength in the institutions of local and state government and voluntary agencies.

And by pursuing these principles, we hope to achieve a society more pluralistic in its operation and more equal in its opportunity, We do not believe that equality of opportunity is the enemy of diversity.

* * *

If we are successful—with our philosophy—in actually bringing about this realignment of power between the levels of government, what sort of nation will we become?

We will no longer be divided by the fear of centralized domination and the personal alienation such domination always brings.

At the same time we will not be a nation where tranquillity and calm and harmony reign supreme. A national nirvana is not in the cards for America.

We have seen what happens in the arena of labor relations when strikes and lockouts and sabotage are replaced by orderly grievance procedures. Labor and management do not become sweethearts; opposing economic forces do not merge their goals. What does happen, in the best of times, is that the force of the antagonism is channeled through an institution that permits progress for all the antagonists.

In the same way, under the New Federalism, the relatively poor will not lose their envy of the rich. The states will not lose their reluctance to cede power to either the local or national government. The federal bureaucracy will not lose its capacity for either initiative or inertia. Tensions will continue to exist, and indeed they should exist—provided we can build those institutions that channel these tensions into progress for all. We are not slicing a pie; we are building a cathedral. Productive tension, the modern descendant of "divine discontent," is the mortar we need to build it.

* * *

One job of government in the final third of this century is to encourage competition among the centers of power without allowing it to become cutthroat competition and without taking the easy way out toward the monopoly of centralization. To abolish all tension would be to lose our freedom; we intend to harness tension and make it productive.

On the basis of the examples I gave you a bit earlier, I believe you can discern a strategy that is being put into action. It may be helpful to those who like to plot our future moves, because the New Federalism approach of this administration has built into government not only credibility but predictability. It will be useful in doing what I said was needed at the beginning of my talk: in criticizing us about how well we do what we have set out to do.

* * *

The credo of the New Federalist, as I see it, is this:

- We must act as one nation in determining national goals.
- We must act as a federation of states and localities in meeting those goals, providing leeway for local options and individual diversity.
- The federal government and the courts must provide checks against any unfairness inflicted by local government, and local government must be able to provide checks against unfairness caused by national standards.
- Power must be permitted to seek its own level of efficient response, flowing to the level of government that is closest to the people and willing and able to exercise it.
- Local innovation and voluntary action must be aggressively encouraged, which limits the liability of the failure of worthwhile experiments and raises the chances of finding practical solutions.
- We must reinstill a new respect for individual responsibility and personal freedom, recognizing that the dignity of work is the counterpart of human dignity.
- The individual citizen must think and act on two levels: He must contribute to the determination of our national goals and then must involve himself locally in making those goals a reality where he lives.

This may not seem like a revolutionary credo, but if it is followed in our time, it could have the same revolutionary impact that followed the acceptance of the ideas of the original Federalists.

* * *

In spelling out the fundamental principles of a new approach to government, I have had to oversimplify. In actual operation, it is infinitely complex—far more complex, I submit, than a doctrinaire liberalism or conservatism.

These are some of the questions we face in putting these principles into practice:

What issues or problems lend themselves to national standards and which do not? For example, air and water pollution, crossing interstate lines, calls for a national approach—and an interstate highway system can hardly be developed on the basis of purely local initiative. On the other hand, a broad range of municipal and state services are better dealt with entirely at that level, assuming that these services can be adequately financed. That is what the president's proposed Revenue Sharing Plan is all about. Nevertheless, the question is a tough one and the answer is as tough, or perhaps complex, as the question itself.

Another complex question: How can we be sure, in the process of decentralization, that the local government can handle the job? To paraphrase a revolutionary slogan, decentralization without preparation is abdication. For example, we know it would be far more effective for local government to administer our manpower training programs. When you sit in Washington and pull the strings, you discover an awful lot of slack in almost every string. On the other hand—there's that phrase again—when you sit in Omaha and a federal program is dumped in your lap, you are not likely to have the organization to make use of it effectively. What we have done in this situation is to set up a phased-in decentralization. Planning money is provided 90 percent by the federal government; as soon as a state shows it has a plan to handle program administration, it gets administrative control of part of the program; as soon as that plan reaches a certain level of success, it earns a larger slice of control, until, at its own pace, it is ready to handle the entire administrative job.

Another complexity: How do we decentralize when local political boundaries make little economic sense? A labor market does not live within city limits, and a transportation system doesn't end at the county line. For this reason, in many cases, we have been encouraging metropolitanism, or regional planning, in an effort to make the political system fit the problems it is called on to meet, and not the other way around.

* * *

Let me conclude with a reference that illustrates in a different way the spirit of the New Federalism.

Those of you who are familiar with industrial relations know about the Hawthorne effect. Some years ago, experiments were conducted at the Hawthorne Works of the Western Electric Company in Chicago. These experiments dealt with the effect of different physical variables on productivity. One of these variables was the intensity of the lighting. The workers were told that the light level of their work area would be raised to see if productivity increased. It was, and it did, resulting in much attention to the experiment and the workers involved. The light was increased some more, and again productivity rose. Then somebody had the bright—or dim—idea of telling them the lighting would be lowered to its original level, and surprisingly enough, productivity still rose. This experience led to the identification of the so-called Hawthorne effect. The level of lighting wasn't nearly as important as the active participation and sense of importance of the workers in the experiment.

I have not told this story merely to revalidate my academic credentials. In government today, we are involving the people in an experiment to replace the deadening "Washington effect" with a constructive Hawthorne effect. The very fact of our effort to try a new approach, a new experiment in government, involving the people in this experiment, should have a stimulating effect of its own and help make that experiment succeed.

That is what we, as a nation, are searching for. When this administration is over—hopefully, not until the year this nation reaches its two hundredth anniversary—we hope to have introduced new standards of fairness, new respect for diversity, and a new spirit of confidence in our system of government.

PRESCRIPTION FOR ECONOMIC POLICY: "STEADY AS YOU GO"

Address delivered by Office of Management and Budget Director George P. Shultz to the Economic Club of Chicago, April 22, 1971.

I have a simple but apparently controversial thesis to present this evening: the basic strategy of economic policy and its current tactical implementation are generally on course, and economic policy can benefit from application of the old nautical phrase "Steady as you go."

For we are *going*—forward with expansion of the economy, as the war in Vietnam continues to wind down, and as the pressures of inflation diminish in their intensity.

But also, with each passing day, the pressures mount to alter the course and to steer not by the compass but by the wind, tossing caution to the wind in the process. I can assure you that these counsels meet strong resistance from the president.

Of course, there are problems. There are uncertainties to be monitored and adjusted for in the tactics of economic policy as new data become available. There are changes in the structure of demand and supply in the marketplace that must be taken into account. Unemployment is too high, and there are pockets of unemployment created mainly by the shift from war to peacetime production that must be treated directly.

But beyond these issues, what are the broad objectives of the president's economic policy?

One strategic purpose of this administration has been to slow a rapidly escalating inflation without inducing a downturn in economic activity.

Another has been to stop the government budget from creating instability, which it had been doing, and get the budget onto a more sustainable basis, which is what we are doing now.

A third has been, and still is, to create the conditions for steady economic expansion in a way that nourishes the freedom and innovative spirit of management, labor, and individuals in a way that does not involve the takeover of the economy by government.

Now, let's look at the results so far.

Inflation has begun a turn downward after a relatively mild slowing of the economy. It has taken longer than we hoped and unemployment has been higher than we wanted, but the progress is unmistakable. The Consumer Price Index, for example, has declined in its rate of increase from over 6 percent in the first half of 1970 to a little under 5 percent in the second half of 1970 to about 2.7 percent in the first quarter of 1971. This is the lowest quarterly increase since the first quarter of 1967.

A balance in the budget at full employment has been attained and held for all three Nixon years after three years of rapidly rising and ultimately tremendous deficits at full employment, thereby removing a destabilizing government influence from the economy and replacing it with a steadying influence.

And now the economy is moving forward, having registered a solid advance of 6.5 percent in real GNP in the first quarter of this year, with the upward movement clearly and substantially stronger and more broadly based toward the end of the quarter than at the beginning.

Yet there are real differences in approach to economic policy today, and we would do well to recognize the disagreements and clarify the arguments.

There is a school of thought that our economy has changed to such an extent that the free market economy will no longer work well enough. In order to achieve stability, this school says, government must do much more to manage the private sector. Some members of this school believe that more government management is needed, not only temporarily to cure our current inflation but indefinitely.

It is time to challenge the basic premise that the economy has changed drastically over the past decade. "Times have changed" is a truism that is hard to refute—but let us see what has changed and what has not.

A principal argument that has been used to justify this seem-ing newness is that corporations and labor now have a great deal more market power than they previously had.

In fact, however, there is little evidence that the power of busi-ness has grown or become more concentrated or monopolistic in recent times. Studies of horizontal integration, which use concen-tration ratios and rates of return, find little evidence of a secular increase in this indicator of monopoly. Likewise, a study of vertical integration, which uses sales to value-added ratios, finds no evi-dence for a secular trend. Monopoly power does not appear to be on the rise.

When conglomeration was in vogue a few years ago, the spec-ter was raised of a dozen supercorporations dominating the busi-ness scene. But because conglomeration did not provide a magic formula for management or financial success, that threat has receded. Waves of conglomerate activity have been experienced in the US economy before. As before, the aftermath of the recent wave has been its reversal. Antitrust enforcement was a factor, but the free market itself provided the main self-cleansing force. The trend in business today is toward more competition, not less, and the successful conglomerates have often been the agents of this sharper competition.

Only in an atmosphere of false boom, of an economy super-heated by government, covering up errors of business judgment, can inefficient aggregations of enterprise prosper. We have now seen what happens when government stops racing the economic engine beyond its capacity to perform: the wheeling and dealing gives way to a more fundamental, and more healthy, form of com-petition among business enterprises.

But what about organized labor? Has it grown in power so markedly in recent years that new regulations are needed in the labor market and in collective bargaining?

Let us look at the government sector of the economy. Here we see both rapid growth in union membership and rapid growth in employment, with the proportion rising from about 12.6 percent to about 18.2 percent of the government labor force over the years from 1956 to 1968. It is noteworthy, but perhaps not surprising under the circumstances, that wage rates have risen especially rapidly in this sector of the economy. In my judgment, the problems of employer-employee relations in government will deserve and will command more and more attention in the years ahead. Certainly, we are far from a resolution of the fundamental problems involved, and they are problems that will affect not only wages and costs—taxes—in the public sector, but the private labor market as well. This is indeed a new factor in the picture.

In the private nonfarm sector of the economy, by sharp contrast, union membership grew only slightly, not nearly as fast as employment, so that its proportionate importance declined from about 38 percent to about 32 percent of this labor force. Lack of growth does not mean a lack of issues about present arrangements in the labor market, but it seems fair to say that the issues are not newly created. It cannot be argued that the current inflation is associated with rising union strength.

Broad statistics on the increase in average hourly earnings of private nonfarm workers show a level of increase that must be reduced if we are to have an extended period of price stability. At the same time, they tend to confirm the picture of no basic change in the arrangements of labor markets. The rise in wages and benefits over twelve-month spans has moved largely within a narrow band between 6 and 8 percent for about five years. There are differential movements by industry, with nonunion areas such as "trade" moving up more sharply when labor markets were at their tightest and reacting more quickly to the current slack. It may be noted that conditions in labor markets did not ease greatly until mid-1970. Conversely, fixed-term contracts tend to produce a slower response in union rates when the labor market tightens but to project that response, unfortunately sometimes at an unwarranted and unwise level, on into a period of changed economic circumstances. This is, however, a well-known phenomenon, identifiable throughout the post–World War II period.

Another well-known movement is also under way, one that has created great difficulty in the fight against inflation but which will now provide some help. The top of a boom and a time of slowing economic activity are always times when the growth of output per man hour—productivity—also slows. But as output rises again, productivity does so as well and initially at a rate above its long-term average. A little-noted but very important aspect of the first quarter results was the appearance again of this predictable development: productivity rose at a rate better than 5 percent after three years of below-average growth. This shift will make a dramatic difference in unit costs of labor and is a hopeful factor insofar as inflation is concerned.

But that is not the main point here. The point is that events are proceeding generally in accord with what might be expected on the basis of past experience.

There are special problems. High expectations for performance of the economy create a dynamic of their own. We have already noted the area of government employment. The construction industry has long been in difficulty and may well be helped out of at least some of its problems through efforts now being made, with stimulation from the president. And there are a number of other industries, notably transportation, where high wage settlements pose difficult cost problems.

The steel industry is very much on our minds. The problem here is not one of setting an inflationary wage pattern: steel is at the end of the round, not the beginning. Nor is the industry so large and important that it can force a generally higher cost level on the economy. The problem is the reverse: the industry is weak, beset with competition from substitute materials, losing ground in world markets, and showing a rate of return that can hardly impress investors. These problems will be facing labor and management whatever the outcome of their wage bargaining and would be badly aggravated by a settlement that extends fixed, high increases into future years.

The answer to these problems is not more severe import quotas, for these will only put American steel users in a poorer and poorer competitive position at home as well as abroad.

Management and labor have a common and severe problem here. Working together with a common goal, they can make a big difference in cost per ton, even without major changes in technology. Perhaps government can help. Certainly a union that produced a Clint Golden [the intellectual steel workers union representative who popularized the idea of employee profit sharing to increase productivity] and a Joe Scanlon [a boxer turned innovative labor relations theorist and representative] can draw upon its traditions for constructive alternatives. We need leadership from the industry to produce a program that combines fair wages and competitive cost through high productivity. In this direction, there is a chance for secure jobs, important to young and older workers alike, and of adequate returns for the capital necessary to the long-run health of the industry.

Two other problem areas deserve special note.

Economic activity in 1970 was substantially disrupted by strikes, which occurred with relatively high frequency. Strikes are unfortunate. Peaceful settlements are certainly to be preferred, and we may expect 1971 to be somewhat more peaceful than its predecessor. But we must also remember that strikes occur most often when an economy is shifting its gears. Last year, when the brakes were applied to inflation, profit margins narrowed, making it difficult for companies to meet the rising demands of labor, demands often reflecting the absence of any gain in real earnings during the prior contract term. The result was conflict. But the fact of this conflict is not evidence that our system is breaking down. It is evidence that the system is working—reacting, as it must, to the end of a spiraling rate of inflation.

Over the past two decades, we have engaged in more and more trade with the rest of the world. The high returns from this increase in trade have been shared by both Americans and foreigners.

In addition, competition from abroad has served to protect the consumer in the United States. The share of the economy represented by trade in goods and services has increased from about 9 percent to over 12 percent of GNP since 1950, with exports growing from about 5 percent to 6.5 percent of the GNP and imports from a little over 4 percent to about 6 percent.

But this increased trade, especially the imports, has posed severe problems in many industries and imposed inequities in some cases. The whole area of international economic policy deserves careful, hard-nosed, and comprehensive review. That review is going forward now under the aegis of the new Council on International Economic Policy, created last February by the president's executive order. The president, who has traveled to sixty-seven countries over the past twenty-four years, is determined that when American business goes abroad, its interests will be strongly represented and advocated by our government.

Perhaps the most troublesome problem from the standpoint of economic policy generally is the area to which I am the closest: the federal budget. The upward thrust built into this gigantic flow of spending is awesome, and there is a continuous and continuing threat that outlays will develop a momentum carrying them well beyond full employment revenues. Tempting though the immediate prospect of such free spending seems to be, it is bad news for the long-run prospects of the economy. Inflation or a tax increase follows in its wake.

For fiscal year 1971, despite a deficit we now estimate at about $19 billion, outlays will be held just within full employment revenues, but only because of the president's willingness to veto apparently popular spending bills and of the willingness of a sufficient number of members of Congress to stand with him.

Fiscal year 1972 will not start for another ten weeks, and Congress has barely started its work on this budget. Yet action so far, other things remaining as in the president's budget, already carry the deficit above $15 billion and outlays to a level well above full employment revenues.

We desperately need a steadiness, a sense of balance, and longer-term perspective in our budget policy. The years 1971 and 1972 are certainly important to this administration, but we must operate also with an eye to 1973 and beyond.

Do we have the ability—perhaps a better word is *guts*—to hold a steady course on the budget? I can assure you of a strong effort from this administration.

The president has been earning the reputation for credibility and perseverance the hard way. When he came into office, he said he would slow the increasing momentum of inflation. Others said the inflationary thrust could never be contained without a virtual takeover of economic activity or a major depression. It was, and without either.

The decisions were not easy to make. The cutbacks required to balance the full-employment budget and the degree of monetary restraint necessary to slow the inflation were not popular. But now we can see a reduction of the rate of inflation.

A portion of the battle against inflation is now over; time and the guts to take the time, not additional medicine, are required for the sickness to disappear. We should now follow a noninflationary path back to full employment, assessing developments as we go and remaining ready to provide stimulation as needed.

But the temptation is there to go overboard on excessive stimulation. These pressures exist on both the monetary and budgetary fronts. We must again provide the steadiness to resist these pressures.

The effects of balanced stimulation appear to be taking hold. Interest rates have fallen sharply, and as is usually the case, new housing starts have increased substantially.

As you all have also read recently, the increase in gross national product from the fourth to the first quarter was the largest absolute increase in history. Although we can't recover from an auto strike every quarter, we expect solid increases in output for the remainder of the year.

These facts, along with a policy of "steady as you go," have been accompanied by an unprecedented rise in the stock market. It was just about a year ago that the president suggested it might be a good time to buy stocks. Stocks are up about 30 percent from the time he made that statement.

The facts reviewed here do not suggest a sharp departure from prior experience. Perhaps the only significant departure is the "steady as you go" policy. A colleague of mine at the University of Chicago, in a recent *Newsweek* column, said the major threat to prudent management of the economy is the "for God's sake, let's do something" philosophy. I think there is a great deal of merit in what he says.

Government does have the responsibility to remove artificial props to wages and prices when the free market system is abused.

And in selective cases, in a critical industry, or in an especially flagrant situation, government should be willing to be the catalyst in achieving voluntary stabilization and, when necessary, helping to restructure the bargaining process.

But we will not be drawn into a series of steps that will lead to wage and price controls, rationing, black markets, and a loss of the effectiveness of the free economic system.

A single theme runs through everything this administration does. In foreign policy, our government will help others help themselves, where they are willing to bear the major portion of their own defense and where it is in our national interest to help. In domestic policy, the federal government is moving to help people more, in a way that returns power and responsibility to states and localities. And in economic policy, the federal government will seek to create the climate in which a free economy can expand steadily and solidly, without domination by government.

There is a consistency to this philosophy, a balanced approach that permits the diffusion of power in the foreign, domestic, and economic areas.

Those of you familiar with sailing know what a telltale is— a strip of cloth tied to a mast to show which way the wind is blowing.

A captain has the choice of steering his ship by the telltale, following the prevailing winds, or steering by the compass.

In a democracy, you must keep your eye on the telltale, but you must set your course by the compass. That is exactly what the president of the United States is doing. The voice from the bridge says, "Steady as you go."

CHAPTER 7

America in the World

We are part of a world with problems and opportunities all around us, whether we like it or not. So how does a government respond to that? I have two examples to share here from my later years as secretary of state that show how these sorts of choices are argued and made in the day-to-day workings of government.

The first is about our position in the world and the sort of ongoing effort needed to support our interests. I had that in mind when I testified before the House Appropriations Committee in 1987 and took those members of Congress on a quick tour around the world, identifying how global engagement made us safer and more prosperous, promoted democratic values, and served a humanitarian purpose. That is as true now as it was then, and I hope that these examples help illustrate that.

But it takes resources—in terms of both money and people—to sustain this. As I said then, "Foreign affairs issues do not lend themselves to quick fixes; Americans have to be prepared to tackle them on a steady, long-term basis." A major responsibility of the executive agency leaders who make up the cabinet is to budget for their needs, submit that to the White House budget director, and then defend that budget request, as submitted by the president, before Congress. Throughout this process, people often disagree. In fact, when

Secretary of State George P. Shultz delivers a speech, "U.S. Foreign Policy: Realism and Progress," at the 37th session of the United Nations General Assembly, New York, on September 30, 1982.
COURTESY HOOVER INSTITUTION LIBRARY & ARCHIVES.

I was the first director of the budget under President Nixon, it was my job to herd cabinet member requests into a consistent proposal that supported the president's priorities.

So years later it fell to me to try to convince Congress to meet President Reagan's increased request for the Department of State after a few years of declines. My motivation in that 1987 testimony, then, was not just to convince them of our strategy but more specifically to show how the administration was using the taxpayers' dollars to achieve those goals, country by country. As you can see, it was a busy time for US foreign policy.

Done all in public, this sort of traditional budgeting process was a good way for the American people to learn what they were buying. It let members of Congress do their primary job as protectors of the purse. And it also forced each agency to be deliberate about their spending so that leaders could represent those requests in good faith. The litany of formula-based "continuing resolution" budgets we've seen in recent years straitjacket agency spending and skirt the important governance responsibilities of prioritization and agenda setting.

Of course, the United States goes out in the world, but the world also comes to us. Today the immigration issue is as hot as it has been in years. But we are not the only ones affected by this. How do we understand what is occurring to us so that we develop a strategy for what we do and do not want from our immigration system?

First we need to recognize that changing demographics, disparate economic growth, wars, and environmental changes have set off a historic global movement of peoples. This will have a profound impact on societies. Richer countries are rapidly aging as fertility declines and life expectancy increases. In fact, population growth in many global powers—the European Union, Japan, Russia, China—has stalled, and workforces are already shrinking. But this is not the case for the United States, Canada, and Australia—all countries with a long history of immigration.

I recall a few years ago, my friend Lee Kuan Yew, the creator of modern Singapore, visited San Francisco. I greeted him, "It's good to see you again. What brings you here?" He replied, "You Americans have created a very interesting innovative atmosphere at Stanford and in Silicon Valley, so I thought I should come over to see if we could learn from you and people in America to use some of your ideas at home. And you can only learn if you are part of something, so we've created a new investment firm here in order to become immersed in this environment." I agreed that it was a good idea but added, "One thing you'll find is that there are people from all over the world here." To this he replied, "I know that, but it could only happen in America." In other words, the United States has a history of attracting a diverse set of people, including the best and the brightest, who contribute in a wide variety of ways.

Meanwhile, most of the future growth in the world's population will come from developing South Asia and Africa, where fertility rates remain high but governance and economic conditions are often poor. Will these people look to our shores, too? What do we as a country want from that, and what might we wish to avoid? In 1988, I shared my thoughts on this topic with the Senate Committee on the Judiciary as part of our own refugee admissions planning process. As you can see, the United States looked out then and saw a world different from the one we see today. But we were optimistic about America's place and capabilities within it.

RESOURCES ARE NEEDED
FOR EFFECTIVE FOREIGN POLICY

Statement by Secretary of State George P. Shultz before the House Appropriations Committee Subcommittee on Foreign Operations, March 11, 1987. Edited for length.

I welcome this opportunity to meet with the committee today because it gives me the opportunity to convey to you my deep concern about perhaps the most urgent but least recognized foreign policy challenge facing us today: the danger of rapidly diminishing resources committed to international affairs.

As we face the third consecutive year of sharp cuts in our foreign affairs budget, I am concerned that the United States—through a series of reductions in people, facilities, and programs overseas—is creating for itself a strategy of retreat. If we fail to deal effectively with this problem, it will directly threaten our ability to exercise coherent and consistent foreign policy leadership in support of our national interests.

I think all Americans can agree on the broad goals of our foreign policy. Put simply, they are to protect our national security, to promote our domestic prosperity, to foster democratic values, to advance our humanitarian ideals, to combat narcotics trafficking, and to thwart terrorism.

Over the last six years, this administration has worked hard toward these objectives. We have made substantial progress toward reinvigorating our economy, restoring our military strength, and strengthening our ties with allies in Europe, Asia, Latin America, and elsewhere.

It has involved a lot of unspectacular but vital spadework in the day-by-day management of our policies by the men and women of the foreign affairs agencies. They have worked to keep Washington informed of developments in other countries and to gain support for US policies. Their contribution is hard to quantify, but it has been essential.

As a result of these efforts on behalf of President Reagan's policies, our European alliance is strong and vital. In NATO,

American efforts to advance peace and progress abroad have been buttressed by a new sense of vitality and common purpose. We have also built a network of strong ties in Asia—relationships that will be crucial to global prosperity and regional security well into the next century.

Through firmness and realism, we have embarked on a new high-level dialogue with the Soviet Union—not just on arms control, but on the full agenda of issues that divide us. And for the first time in history, we now have the prospect of negotiating substantial reductions in the nuclear arsenals of both sides. In the case of intermediate-range nuclear forces, progress toward agreement has recently been accelerated by our tabling of a draft treaty in Geneva and by the Soviet decision no longer to link an INF [intermediate-range nuclear forces] agreement to the resolution of other arms control issues.

In the developing world, we have worked to support a remarkable surge toward democracy, most notably in Latin America, where the percentage of the population living under freely elected governments has grown from 30 percent in 1979 to more than 90 percent today. Democracy has also made great strides in the Philippines, in the Caribbean, and throughout the Third World. More and more people seem willing to resist authoritarian or military governments and the yoke of totalitarian oppressors; they seek and deserve our help.

We have also seen an encouraging trend toward greater confidence in market–oriented solutions to the problems of economic growth. We now find, almost everywhere in the world, movements to decentralize, deregulate, and denationalize. At the UN Special Session on Africa last May, the African nations committed themselves to more open markets and less state intervention. Even in Communist countries, there is growing recognition that entrepreneurial initiative in a market environment is the engine of development and growth.

All of this represents important progress. But there is still much to be done. Precisely because foreign affairs issues do not lend themselves to quick fixes, Americans have to be prepared to tackle them on a steady, long-term basis. Yet just as we should be consolidating and building upon our recent gains, we stand on the threshold of a major reversal brought about by penny-wise, pound-foolish budget decisions.

Last January, President Reagan submitted to Congress a request for foreign operations appropriations for FY '87 that represented a sound and prudent investment in our national interest. The request came within a larger budget for international affairs activities that amounted to less than two cents on every dollar in the proposed federal budget, which itself was within the new Gramm-Rudman ceilings.

Yet the resources provided under the congressional budget resolution for FY '87 were 20 percent less than the amount requested. This reduced our foreign affairs operating base by $1.8 billion, or 20 percent, from the actual FY 1986 levels. After accommodating earmarked items that had to be funded, the effective cut for the bulk of our operations was more on the order of 50 percent. This was on top of the $1.5 billion cut from prior year levels that we suffered in the FY '86 congressional appropriations process, meaning that over the past two years, we lost over $3.3 billion from the resources we were operating with in FY '85. These cuts were more severe, in percentage terms, that any other function in the administration's budget requests.

These cuts threaten our vital interests not just in one or two regions but around the globe. They threaten the stability of our allies. They threaten our war on terrorists. They threaten our attempt to promote democratic values and reforms. They threaten our efforts to expand and develop trade.

And they threaten our ability both to understand and influence developments in a dynamic international environment—make no mistake about it. Though a small part of the international affairs budget, whether or not we can maintain a sound foreign affairs infrastructure will determine in large part whether we can successfully pursue a coherent, sound, and strong foreign policy. In short, by attempting to save the country some dollars over the short run, these cuts threaten to cost us much more—in money, in jobs, even in lives—over the long run.

The president's foreign affairs budget might usefully be looked upon as a form of national insurance. In asking the Congress to devote only two cents out of every budget dollar to our foreign policy goals, the president has determined the minimum premium we must pay as a people to safeguard the peace and lead the free world. Those who would cut the foreign affairs budget even further are gambling needlessly with our nation's future.

No one can say for sure how large the gamble will be. We know we pay some price every day in terms of lost opportunities to influence events. Perhaps a crisis that could have been averted today by timely and relatively inexpensive military or economic assistance, or through diplomatic efforts, will explode in our faces the day after tomorrow. . . .

* * *

As a former budget director, I know firsthand the difficult and painful decisions you face in attempting to reduce the federal budget deficit. It is a goal shared by the president and me. This budget reflects a number of painful choices we had to make as part of our contribution to the deficit reduction target.

We had to pare down and even eliminate programs that, under other circumstances, would have great merit. Our proposed program level for the Andean countries, for example, is far below the optimum when you consider our interests and their needs. In Korea, rather than a brusque cutoff from a large FMS [foreign military sales] credit program, it would have been helpful to provide some transition to strict commercial terms. I could cite many other examples of programs cut substantially below the amount my program managers considered necessary. The point is, Mr. Chairman, this budget is not a wish list. At each stage of the budget review process we asked this question: How can we justify these investments in an age of fiscal restraint? I hope my testimony will answer that question to your satisfaction.

My colleagues and I recognize that we will not get very far without the cooperation of the Congress. We are committed to work with Congress. We welcome your close scrutiny of our budget proposals, and we will do our best to respond to all of your questions in a forthright and timely manner to the best of our ability.

Let me now provide you with some concrete examples of how our resource requests help promote our objectives.

National Security

Let's start with our national security.

We live in a dangerous world, and we face the choice of defending ourselves alone—and I might add, at tremendous cost—or working with allies who share our values and who face the same enemies we do. We have chosen the latter course.

Our country's alliances are based on a sharing of risks and responsibilities. The Soviet challenge is global. Its military machine stands poised down the middle of Europe, pursues its invasion of neighboring Afghanistan, and actively arms and supports repressive regimes in Eastern Europe, Indochina, Ethiopia, Cuba, and Nicaragua.

Some of our allies lack the resources to provide for their own security concerns while simultaneously responding to the basic economic needs of their own people. Because we know they must do both if they are to survive and grow, we must help them finance the modernization of their armed forces. Over the years we have made commitments to do so. Yet the resources made available this past year fall far short of these commitments. For example, in FY '87 we have had to slash aid to Spain by 73 percent. The story is repeated for Portugal, Turkey, Greece, and even the Philippines, where we had to reduce the military assistance program by 50 percent.

Such reductions raise fundamental doubts about US dependability and risk the loss of vital military and port facilities.

Without these allies and their facilities, we would have to spend a great deal more on defense and have many more of our citizens under arms. . . .

Promoting US Prosperity

Let me turn now to the second goal of US foreign policy: promoting domestic prosperity. Americans usually suppose that their prosperity is largely determined by the monetary and fiscal policies we pursue at home; the fact is, however, that economic conditions abroad have a crucial impact on the health of the American economy. Our representatives abroad are on the front line when it comes to understanding these conditions and influencing other nations to avoid taking steps that would adversely affect US prosperity. A third of our manufactured exports, for example, goes to the Third World, which also buys about 40 percent of our agricultural exports. These countries have accounted for more than half of the growth in US exports since 1975. At this juncture, approximately one out of every twenty workers in our manufacturing plants and one out of every five acres of our farmland produce for Third World markets. I might add that two out of every five acres of our farmland produce for export. That's how interrelated our farm community is with the international community.

Economic stagnation in parts of the developing world has vividly—if painfully—highlighted these relationships. Economic growth in many developing countries is weak. Partly as a result, our exports to these countries—which were increasing at more than 30 percent a year in the late 1970s—have tapered off.

For example, between 1981 and 1985, the countries of Latin America and the Caribbean experienced a sharp decline in their real incomes. Our exports to that region during the same period dropped by over $12 billion—equivalent to 300,000 jobs. There's a direct correlation.

It has long been obvious that by promoting economic development we make a direct contribution to our own nation's economic well-being. For example, in 1960, Turkey's per capita income was about $500; Pakistan's was barely $100 per year. By 1985, both countries had more than doubled their incomes and had become major purchasers of US products. Between 1979 and 1985, US exports to Pakistan doubled; to Turkey, they nearly quadrupled. So, I think you can see, our assistance serves a hard interest in strengthening countries that provide growing markets for US goods.

I hope these illustrations make clear that to improve our own long-term economic prospects, we must promote economic growth in the developing countries. It was with such ends in mind that we initiated a comprehensive plan—the Baker Plan—to get developing countries on a path of sustained economic growth. The Baker Plan calls for bold economic reforms to be supported by the multilateral banks, the private sector, and bilateral aid. For the major debtor countries, the plan calls for substantial increases in commercial bank lending and in loans from the World Bank and from bilateral donors.

For the low-income countries, mainly in sub-Saharan Africa, IDA [International Development Association] funds, special IMF [International Monetary Fund] funds, and bilateral grants would be used for this creative effort.

But last year, the first year the plan was operative, our funding request for the multilateral banks was cut by a third. Similarly, bilateral funds were slashed to a level where we could only provide 30 percent of the resources necessary to support economic policy reforms in Africa. Clearly, it wasn't only foreign nationals who were hurt by these cuts. All those Americans whose livelihood depends on exports to the Third World were hurt as well. And I need scarcely remind you of the consequences to our domestic banking system—and indeed, the entire world financial system—should major overseas debtors be thrown into default.

The cuts in our support for the World Bank and the other multilateral banks are especially costly. These institutions are just about the most cost-effective tools we have for leveraging resources from other wealthy countries for our friends and trading partners in Africa, Asia, and Latin America. For example, the United States puts up only a small fraction of the funds mobilized by the World Bank. For every dollar the US contributes to the International Development Association, the World Bank's affiliate for aiding the poorest countries, other countries contribute three.

Conversely, when the United States fails to follow through on its commitments, this reduces the World Bank's lending capacity far more than the actual cut in US support. . . .

Promoting Democratic Values

The US also has a vital stake in promoting democratic values and institutions. This isn't starry-eyed idealism; it is realism. Democratic nations respect the rule of law both domestically and in foreign affairs; they grow more rapidly, and they are more stable internally, more capable of resisting subversion through their own efforts.

Thus, in promoting democratic values and human rights, we are protecting our security and prosperity as well as advancing our most fundamental ideals. . . .

Humanitarianism

Let me turn to another broad goal of American foreign policy: our humanitarian efforts. The American people can be justifiably proud of their humanitarian instincts. Over the past few years the assistance we have provided has meant the difference between life and death for literally millions of Africans who faced the worst drought and famine the continent has experienced in this century. During the height of this crisis, the United States provided 2.2 million metric tons of food aid at a cost of over one billion dollars; another $150 million was spent to provide medicines, shelter, wells, and the other immediate needs for those worst affected by the drought. This was in addition to the regular economic assistance we provided during the same period. . . .

Our assistance to the world refugee population is especially noteworthy. In the six fiscal years since the passage of the Refugee Act of 1980, the American people have offered new homes to more than half a million refugees—a population greater than that for all other resettlement countries combined. Our position as the acknowledged leader in assisting the world's refugees—the victims of oppression in their own homelands—is further demonstrated in our generous financial support to multilateral and bilateral refugee relief programs. The strong, sustained interest of the congressional committees that oversee these programs has enabled the United States to contribute annually more than 25 percent of the international community's total contribution to the world's more than ten million refugees.

But it seems to me that what we all seek is the end of the conditions that create the need for many of these emergency programs in the first place. Obviously, we cannot eliminate natural disasters, but we do have the ability, the moral imperative, and the national interest to confront the man-made causes of poverty and repression.

Our development assistance programs do just that—attack the causes of human affliction. Political, economic, and social turmoil causes vast numbers of people to flee their homelands. Conversely, the development of democracy and expanded economic opportunity can dramatically reduce the numbers of people who find a need to abandon their native lands. Clearly, it is in our national interest, as well as our humanitarian tradition, to tackle these problems with resolve. . . .

Combatting Terrorism

I need not belabor the threat of terrorism before this audience. In 1985, the last full year for which we have detailed analysis, we counted nearly 800 international terrorist incidents. A third of those incidents caused casualties, with over 800 killed and 1,200 wounded.

These figures tend to understate the actual level of terrorist activity, since incidents confined to one country, with the nationals of only one country involved, are not included.

Although I by no means exclude the use of force from our list of options, there is more to an aggressive counterterrorist policy than using force against terrorists. We must and do work with other nations to identify, track, apprehend, prosecute, and punish terrorists. This requires that we

- closely cooperate with other nations on counterterrorism efforts;

- persuade those nations reluctant to cooperate in combatting international terrorism; and
- provide training and other assistance to those with the will but not the means. . . .

Conclusion

Mr. Chairman, I hope my presentation today has helped to clarify just how the foreign assistance budget enables us to pursue our specific national interests. We in the administration and you in the Congress must make many difficult choices in these times of severe fiscal restraint. But as I pointed out at the outset of my testimony, over the past two years Congress has reduced the foreign affairs budget far too drastically. Unless we take action now to reverse current trends, many foreign policy gains we have made in recent years could be wiped out.

What, then, must be done to narrow the gap between our interests and our capacity to pursue them? Well, the obvious first step is to restore the funds that have been cut and review the obstacles to using our funds as effectively as possible. But we must do something more. We must also relearn two old and very important lessons—lessons that were well understood forty years ago but are in danger of being forgotten today.

The fundamental lesson is that it takes resources—modest but sustained, applied credibly over time—to advance the national interests of the United States. The expenditure of such resources is not a "giveaway"; it is an investment in a better future for ourselves and our children.

How do US resources advance American interests abroad? The Marshall Plan is a dramatic example. Designed to restore a war-ravaged Europe and prevent the spread of Communism, the plan cost American taxpayers about $14 billion. When it was first proposed in 1947, critics of the plan argued that it was wrong to use taxpayers' money for Europe's internal needs, but their opposition was overcome—and rightly so. Today it is clear that the Marshall

Plan was not simply an act of charity on an unprecedented scale. It also saved Western Europe from Soviet domination—and saved the United States from the disastrous consequences that a Soviet-dominated Europe would have had on our national security, our economic prosperity, and our democratic values.

The success of the Marshall Plan forty years ago demonstrates that, more often than not, the most effective way of promoting our basic goals is by working with others to achieve their basic goals. That is what a Democratic president and a Republican Congress understood in 1947 when they allocated eleven cents out of every federal dollar to fund the Marshall Plan.

And that is what I hope you will all bear in mind as you consider the president's request to allocate only two cents out of every federal dollar to the current foreign affairs budget.

Let me conclude by taking note of a happy coincidence. This year marks the bicentennial of the Constitution and the fortieth anniversary of the Marshall Plan. Both of these milestones should lead us to pause and reflect on the nature and purposes of American government. The bicentennial reminds us that it is possible to establish a government powerful enough to meet its global responsibilities, yet sufficiently constrained to be able to safeguard the rights of individual citizens. The Marshall Plan reminds us that when such a government has a clear sense of purpose and is not paralyzed by internal divisions, it can change the course of world history for the better. That government, of course, is *our* government, and today, as in the past, it is still within our power to change the course of world history for the better.

The opportunities are there. We need only grasp them.

PROPOSED REFUGEE ADMISSIONS FOR FY 1989

Statement by Secretary of State George P. Shultz before the Senate Committee on the Judiciary, Washington, DC, September 18, 1988. Edited for length.

I am pleased to be here this morning once more to present the president's proposal for refugee admissions for fiscal year (FY) 1989. During my tenure as secretary, I have taken particular pride in testifying before this committee about one of the most satisfying foreign policy endeavors the United States undertakes: our assistance to refugees.

It is customary to discuss US aid to refugees in the context of the humanitarian purposes of our foreign policy. Indeed, humanitarianism is the principal motive behind our programs on refugee issues. Yet it is worth emphasizing at the outset of these remarks that we have benefited greatly as a nation by opening our doors to the displaced and politically oppressed. We know from generations of experience that every wave of refugees to have come to our shores has made enormous contributions to all sectors of our society. Just look at those who fled from Nazi Germany, from the Soviet Union, from Indochina, and from Cuba. The contributions to this nation from the refugees who have sought sanctuary here are incalculable. Thus, US refugee policy is an area where our ideals, our humanitarian instincts, and our interests coincide.

I would like to review with you today the principles that have shaped this administration's refugee assistance and admissions policies and the accomplishments that have come from the programs we have pursued. I then want to cover briefly the major refugee issues we face today and also summarize the situation that prompted the emergency consultations in April which led us to increase the admissions ceiling for Eastern Europe and the Soviet Union. Finally, I will present the president's proposal for refugee admissions in fiscal year 1989. . . .

Resources

Before I address specific refugee issues, I want to say a word about resources. There are limited resources available for the foreign affairs budget of the United States. At the same time, there are increased refugee needs, both for assistance and admissions overseas. Final action has not yet been taken on the FY 1989 foreign assistance appropriations for the refugee program. The conference on that bill will occur next week. I urge the conferees to remove the earmarks in both the House and Senate bills. If all of these earmarks at the president's requested funding level became law, over half of the Migration and Refugee Assistance appropriation would be earmarked, and the unmarked programs—which provide lifesaving support to refugees in camps in Africa, Latin America, the Near East, and Southeast Asia—would have to be cut by 25 percent across the board to absorb the increase outside the request level. We need to drop the earmarks on both the regular and the emergency refugee accounts.

Refugee Assistance Policy

About two-thirds of refugee funds help provide the most basic food, shelter, medical care, education or training, and protection for people in camps who have fled human rights abuses, famine, civil war, or invasions. Today the vast majority of the nearly 13 million refugees are found in Asian and African countries. International refugee assistance bolsters these countries' resolve to continue to welcome asylum seekers. The United States has a long-standing tradition of providing diplomatic leadership and substantial financial resources to ensure protection and care and maintenance programs for refugees in camps overseas.

As political conditions permit, this assistance enables thousands of refugees to return to their countries of origin. This solution requires political conditions that are, unfortunately, not foreseeable in the near term for the majority of the world's refugees.

US refugee assistance in first-asylum nations is made more efficient by combining it with the resources of other nations through international refugee assistance organizations. We concentrate our refugee program resources on these international assistance programs, spending about twice as much on the 99 percent of refugees who remain overseas as we do to resettle the refugees admitted each year to the United States.

Refugee Admissions Policy

Our refugee admissions policy reflects the oft-quoted words of Emma Lazarus on the Statue of Liberty. To the "poor, huddled masses yearning to breathe free," we want to offer the same opportunities for a new home in a new land that were extended to our own forefathers. The Refugee Act of 1980 defines whom we may admit as refugees. Each year we must make choices concerning which refugees we admit and in what numbers. These decisions follow naturally from our refugee admissions policy, which provides resettlement when repatriation or local resettlement is not possible or first asylum is not secure.

There are four significant objectives of our admissions policy.

First, each year, in cooperation with the UNHCR [UN High Commissioner for Refugees], refugees who face perilous protection problems in their countries of first asylum are resettled quickly and quietly. Released political prisoners, as from Cuba, are also resettled. We hope soon to begin resettling large numbers of Vietnamese reeducation center detainees as well.

Second, our willingness to resettle refugees encourages other nations to maintain responsible policies of first asylum. This applies not only in Southeast Asia but also in Western Europe, which has a long tradition of offering asylum.

Third, we have a special, ongoing commitment to offer resettlement to refugees overseas who have family in the United States or close ties here through employment or education. Whenever possible, we reduce refugee admissions numbers by channeling family reunion cases through regular immigration channels. The long waiting periods for immigrant visas and the difficulties under which refugees exist overseas do not allow, however, for easy switching of refugees onto an immigrant track.

The fourth objective of our admissions policy is to deter refugees from jeopardizing their own safety by ensuring an orderly flow of refugees through special negotiated direct-departure programs. Such programs also ensure that persons who do not qualify for refugee admission are not stranded in a third country.

Reagan Era Accomplishments in Refugee Affairs

When President Reagan took office, the refugee act was not yet a year old. The successful implementation of this legislation, which weighs the individual's claim to persecution more heavily than any other factor in refugee determinations, is a significant accomplishment of the Reagan years and, I might say, an accomplishment that proceeded with very strong bipartisan support. It's been a very fine program from that and other points of view.

Southeast Asia

Let me first turn to Southeast Asia. Worldwide, our overriding priority in the 1980s has been assisting and resettling Indochinese refugees. We began by processing refugees on beaches as they stepped off boats or swam to shore from sinking crafts. Working closely with our voluntary agency partners, since FY 1981, we have processed and admitted over 400,000 Indochinese refugees—37,000 Highland Lao, 60,000 Lowland Lao, 116,000 Cambodians, and 200,000 Vietnamese.

We recently proposed a comprehensive package of measures designed to dissuade people from the dangers of clandestine departure while preserving the principle of first asylum. A comprehensive solution depends, in part, on a concerted effort of the Southeast Asian nations, Hong Kong, and the resettlement nations to urge the government of Vietnam to expand further the Orderly Departure

Program (ODP). The effective operation of legitimate national screening programs monitored by the UNHCR would ensure that bona fide refugees are recognized and given first asylum. Those deemed not to be refugees should be cared for by the international community until they can return safely to their homes. Refugees should have the opportunity to apply for resettlement, and resettlement countries must continue to offer hope for a new life to these victims of persecution through generous resettlement programs. The United States has by far the strongest resettlement commitment to Indochinese refugees. We have maintained that steady commitment since 1975 and will continue to do so in the future. . . .

Thai-Cambodian Border. In the wake of the fall of the Pol Pot regime, hundreds of thousands of fearful Cambodians fled toward Thailand for food and medical care. Once there, hundreds died from exhaustion due to severe malnutrition or disease. American officials and private citizens provided emergency care to help these people, and the United States has continued since then to provide assistance through the UN Border Relief Operation (UNBRO). We support UNBRO and ICRC [International Committee of the Red Cross] initiatives across the board to improve protection and education for these 300,000 Cambodians.

Latin America and the Caribbean

Mariel Migration Agreement. A major accomplishment of recent years is the Migration Agreement of 1984 with Cuba, which finally put an end to the history of the 1980 Mariel boatlift by encompassing a return of excludable Cubans to Havana. Under the resumed Migration Agreement, we expect to resettle approximately three thousand Cuban political prisoners and family members annually through the refugee program and the attorney general's parole authority. We will continue to consider for admission all political prisoners who wish to apply.

Salvadoran Refugee Repatriations. During the past year, the Central American refugee situation has been alleviated somewhat by the voluntary repatriation of more than 6,700 Salvadoran refugees from camps in Honduras through arrangements monitored by the UNHCR. The latest group returned to El Salvador in mid-August, and there are indications that further repatriations may occur in the future.

Africa

By far the largest refugee emergencies involving life and death have been in Africa. In the past eight years, the Reagan administration has taken the lead in the multilateral responses to crises involving millions of refugees from nineteen different African nations.

Ethiopia. With respect to Ethiopia, currently we are deeply concerned by the refugee problems that threaten war-torn and famine-stricken Ethiopia—for many years a country better known for producing refugees than for absorbing them. Over 300,000 refugees from the civil war in southern Sudan have poured into Ethiopia. In addition, over 400,000 refugees have fled armed conflict between government forces and rebels in northern Somalia. We are working with the UN agencies and other donors to avoid a major humanitarian disaster.

Mozambique. The department's report on the situation of Mozambican refugees in southern Africa underlines the need to pay heed to refugee populations as we consider our policy alternatives in any region of the world. Malawi has been overwhelmed by over 600,000 Mozambican refugees, but the people of Malawi and President Banda have reinforced their solid humanitarian reputation by accepting the presence of this enormous burden.

Near East and South Asia

Afghanistan. There are more than three million Afghan refugees in Pakistan—the largest refugee population in the world. Since 1979, the United States has provided over $600 million in refugee assistance, including over $370 million worth of food. The late President Zia-ul-Haq and the people of Pakistan have offered their land and their hospitality to Afghan refugees for nearly a decade. Now these refugees appear to have the possibility of returning to their homes in the near future. There are obstacles to that repatriation—including the critical danger of land mines strewn throughout Afghanistan by Soviet military forces—but we hope a large number of the Afghan refugees will be able to return home in the coming year.

Palestinian Refugees. The oldest continuing refugee population involves the Palestinian refugees in the Near East. The UN Relief and Works Agency for Palestine Refugees in the Near East (UNRWA) continues to provide basic educational, medical, and relief services to Palestinian refugees in Lebanon, Syria, Jordan, the West Bank, and Gaza. It is vital that UNRWA continue providing services, especially in the West Bank and Gaza. I salute the dedicated staff of UNRWA and, especially, Robert Dillon, the American deputy director general who is leaving that organization after four years of energetic and compassionate service.

Emergency Consultations in FY 1988 and Proposed Refugee Admissions for FY 1989

Throughout the Reagan administration, and consistently since World War II, the United States has vigorously championed the cause of freedom of emigration from the Soviet Union. In the past year, after an eight-year period of only minimal and unacceptable emigration, the Soviet Union has granted exit permits to tens of thousands of persons—primarily Jews, Armenians, ethnic Germans, and some Pentecostalists. All other Soviet citizens, however, have virtually no opportunity to emigrate.

We applaud the emigration policy reforms in the Soviet Union, but we urge the Soviet government to comply fully with the emigration provisions of the Helsinki Final Act. International human rights standards recognize the right to emigrate and to return to one's country but not to immigrate into any country of one's choosing. Standards and limits to immigration are determined by national decision and legislation. The United States has responded generously, but we, too, have limits set by the immigration and refugee laws relating both to eligibility criteria and to the numbers we can absorb.

Two fundamental issues have emerged from this experience with Soviet resettlement.

One is budgetary. In a time of severely constrained budgets, how do we ensure that we will have adequate resources to support an unexpected outflow of emigrants from the Soviet Union without damaging other critical foreign policy programs?

The second is legal. Can all Soviet emigrants be admitted under the refugee provisions of the Immigration and Nationality Act? With the commencement of INS [Immigration and Naturalization Service] processing in Moscow, INS has confirmed that not all potential emigrants meet the statutory definition of *refugee* under the act. We must, therefore, seek alternate immigration channels for those who do not meet the statutory definition in order to offer realistic options to such persons.

We learned this year that there are occasions when our foreign policy goals—encouragement of liberalized emigration policy, for one—dictate a need for flexibility in order to admit groups of people who do not immediately or neatly fit into current immigrant or refugee categories. Unfortunately, such flexibility is not currently available in immigration law. We believe that greater flexibility is an urgent foreign policy and humanitarian need, which we would like to address, together with Congress, over the coming months. One possibility would be a new category of immigrant visa. Including the $140 million earmark for admissions, we will have new funds to admit 82,000 refugees and Amerasian immigrants. That is the Senate version. In addition, we estimate that carryover funds from the FY 1988 dire emergency supplemental will be available to fund an additional 2,000 refugee admissions. Therefore, the potential fully funded admissions level is between 70,500 and 84,000, depending on the final appropriation. With regard to fully funded admissions, at no time will we operate at a rate higher than that for which funds are available in the Migration and Refugee Assistance account.

Establishing the ceiling requires balancing our humanitarian and foreign policy goals, refugee eligibility requirements, domestic resettlement capacity, and estimated costs. For FY 1989, therefore, despite my misgivings and my desire to be absolutely clear to the Congress and not to mislead anyone about actual admissions levels, we are proposing an aggregate, worldwide ceiling for refugee and Amerasian immigrant admissions of 94,000. It comprises three elements:

- up to 84,000 fully funded admissions—that's on the assumption we get the positive numbers that I outlined here;
- up to 6,000 that would be partially funded by HHS [the Department of Health and Human Services], as they are appropriated up to 90,000, and partially by the private sector; and
- up to 4,000 reserved for the separate, private sector program.

The 6,000 partially funded numbers will cover a group of persons some of whom would be eligible for HHS-funded benefits and some who could be admitted without any federal funding whatsoever. Therefore we are not seeking additional federal funds to finance these 6,000 admissions. In addition, we propose to continue the current allocation of 4,000 numbers for the fully privately funded admissions initiative. This private sector initiative has already benefited hundreds of Cuban refugees in fiscal year 1988.

Once the final appropriations for FY 1989 are enacted, we will advise Congress of the operational plan, by region, that is consistent with the actual funding available. If the final appropriations level for the Department of State budget would fund 70,500 admissions in FY 1989, then we would commence the year at an operational level of 70,500. If the final appropriations for FY 1989 fully funds 84,000 admissions in the Department of State budget and 90,000 admissions in the HHS budget, we would commence the fiscal year with an operational plan for 90,000. . . .

Last year, during both the regular and the emergency consultations, we set refugee admissions numbers that were higher than the funds available for the admissions program. This led to confusion and disappointment as the year went on and the money ran out. I am, therefore, very reluctant to begin the fiscal year with an admissions ceiling higher than that for which funds will be available. . . .

Conclusion

So while I have provided a brief justification of the levels we would like to see established as the refugee admissions ceilings, I acknowledge that, at present, we cannot predict what funding will be available to admit these refugees. As the stewards of our refugee policy, however, the administration is responsible for ensuring that our highest humanitarian and foreign policy objectives are reflected in our refugee programs. Let me assure you that we will endeavor to carry out that responsibility to the best of our ability. With the bipartisan support of Congress, we will continue in our traditional humanitarian spirit to provide for the needs of refugees around the world.

A Balanced Approach
to Climate Change

A Balanced Approach to Climate Change

It's become a simple matter of observation that the world is getting warmer, and the consequences are already clear. Tropical diseases are moving north, a new ocean is being created in the Arctic, the ice cap over Greenland is melting, and coral reefs are disappearing, with an important impact on the food chain. Reducing carbon emissions to dampen the rate of increase in the world's temperature is a new sort of governance problem for the United States.

So far, we haven't really come to the point of compromise in this country in thinking about climate policies. Each side demonizes the other and uses the issue as a bludgeon to appeal to their own supporters. A long-term, politically survivable approach is probably going to be one in which each side feels they have given up something that is important to them, but one they also feel is better than the alternatives. Those alternatives—complex and costly regulations on one side or unmitigated climate impacts on the other—are becoming ever more apparent, so maybe that will force the issue before too long.

I think about our approach to a similar, if somewhat simpler, global environmental problem we faced during President Reagan's administration: the deleterious impact of CFC (chlorofluorocarbon) emissions on the global ozone layer.

Secretary of State George P. Shultz
with President Ronald Reagan in the Oval Office.
THE WHITE HOUSE.

Ultimately, the United States led a successful international coalition in dealing with that. Like today, there were doubters then on the science of the problem and our ability to come up with acceptable solutions. President Reagan's "insurance policy," which I describe in the essay that follows, acknowledged those genuine concerns while taking an approach that was broadly palatable, even to them. Importantly, we approached the response in a way that was acceptable to the American industries that would be most impacted by it.

As that essay explains, I favor a new, two-part "insurance policy" approach to today's much larger climate change issue, too. First is sustained public and private support for clean energy research. Since I first studied this issue as head of a cabinet task force on oil import controls in 1969 for President Nixon, the history of public investment in energy R&D has been like a roller coaster. The oil price goes up, and people get interested. It falls, and R&D funding gets cut off. Today the United States spends around seven billion dollars annually on all forms of energy research, and that attracts additional private sector research funding, which at least doubles the amount. I think of the profound importance of research and development to all parts of our society since the Second World War. If we can sustain and gradually grow that energy R&D investment, I am confident that our top-class American scientists and engineers will produce better and cheaper options to deal with the very thorny technical question of emissions reductions—game changers. As we used to say when I was managing the federal budget, the amount in question is a rounding error.

The second part of my climate "insurance policy" is a way to level the playing field so that these new technologies being created have a fair shot at making it in the market. And that is a broad-based revenue-neutral carbon tax. The carbon tax would make polluters pay for what they freely put up into the air today, an approach economists tend to like. But doing that would increase the prices of many of the things we buy and use today. So that's why we propose giving back all the money that the tax collects as a flat per capita rebate. The tax would still encourage people and businesses to emit less carbon, but the check in the mail would lessen the overall economic burden—particularly for those with lower incomes. Meanwhile, we could do away with the many costly mandates and regulations we are already starting to see in the energy arena, which could stunt our economic growth.

In this chapter, I've included an op-ed describing the effort I've undertaken along with James Baker, my successor as secretary of state and a personal friend from Texas. The idea is gradually gaining interest, and we also get plenty of criticism from both sides of the aisle—so I take that as a good first step as far as a workable compromise might go.

A REAGAN APPROACH TO CLIMATE CHANGE

Originally published in the Washington Post *on March 13, 2015.*

The trend of disappearing summer sea ice in the Arctic is clear even though there is always some variability from year to year. Severe winter weather underscores the importance of keeping track of significant trends. Here are the numbers, according to Julienne Stroeve of the National Snow and Ice Data Center in Boulder, Colorado, as reported in the *Economist* in February:

"Between 1953 and 2014, the average area of the Arctic sea ice shrank by 48,000 square kilometers a year."

"Between 1979 and 2014, it shrank by 87,000 square kilometers a year."

"Between 1996 and 2014, the rate rose to 148,000 square kilometers."

The accelerating rate is explained in part by the fact that ice reflects sunlight, but water, which is darker, absorbs it. So as water replaces ice, more heat is retained. Heat transported from lower latitudes could also be part of the explanation.

The picture in Greenland is more complicated, but it is important in the long run. Arctic ice is already in the water, so melting there won't make much of an impact on sea levels. Greenland, though, is home to the world's second-largest land ice mass. Two satellites measure annual melting in Greenland; over the past two decades its net ice loss has been about 140 billion tons per year, and that rate has almost doubled in more recent years. The story is similar in West Antarctica, where surface geography makes it easier for large segments of its ice sheet to slide into a warming ocean. Altogether, we can observe that sea levels are now rising about three millimeters per year. We can also observe that the last time the earth warmed by a few degrees—120,000 years ago—sea levels were at least five meters higher than today.

Temperatures vary. You may have read about a global "stall" in temperature increase over the past decade, despite carbon dioxide levels rising at about 0.5 percent each year. Here again, though, trends tell the bigger story. We know that since humans started to produce more CO_2 in the late 1800s, overall land and ocean temperatures have increased about one degree Celsius, and in Antarctica, teams examining the world's oldest ice cores recently released their findings of 800,000 years of climate history. "Even when our climate was in some other phase, some different way of balancing the many subtle influences that make up the wind and weather and warmth we experience, temperature and greenhouse gases still marched in lockstep," wrote Gabrielle Walker in her book *Antarctica: An Intimate Portrait of a Mysterious Continent.* "Higher temperature always went with higher CO_2. Lower temperature went with lower CO_2."

These are simple and clear observations, so I conclude that the globe is warming and that carbon dioxide has something to do with that fact. Those who say otherwise will wind up being mugged by reality.

I am also impressed by an experience I had in the mid-1980s. Many scientists thought the ozone layer was shrinking. There were doubters, but everyone agreed that if it happened, the result would be a catastrophe. Under these circumstances, President Ronald Reagan thought it best not to argue too much with the doubters but include them in the provision of an insurance policy. With the very real potential for serious harm, US industry turned on its entrepreneurial juices, and the DuPont company developed a set of replacements for the chemicals implicated in the problem along a reasonable time frame and at a reasonable cost. It came up with something that could be done then—not some aspirational plan for 2050. Action is better than aspiration. As matters turned out, the action worked and became the basis for the Montreal Protocol, widely regarded as the world's most successful environmental treaty. In retrospect, the scientists who were worried were right, and the Montreal Protocol came along in the nick of time. Reagan called it a "monumental achievement."[10]

We all know there are those who have doubts about the problems presented by climate change. But if these doubters are wrong, the evidence is clear that the consequences, while varied, will be mostly bad, some catastrophic. So why don't we follow Reagan's example and take out an insurance policy?

First, let's have significant and sustained support for energy research and development. More of that is going on right now than in any previous period. The costs to the federal budget are small—little more than a rounding error—and a serious government effort would attract private capital from investors who want to know what's new and want to contribute. These efforts are producing results. For example, we can now produce electricity from the wind and the sun at close to the same price we pay for electricity from other sources, and we may soon know how to do cost-effective large-scale storage of electricity, thus greatly reducing the intermittency problems of solar and wind and producing a hedge against the great vulnerability of our power grid.

Second, let's level the playing field for competing sources of energy so that costs imposed on the community are borne by the sources of energy that create them, particularly carbon dioxide. A carbon tax, starting small and escalating to a significant level on a legislated schedule, would do the trick. I would make it revenue-neutral, returning all net funds generated to the taxpayers so that no fiscal drag results and the revenue would not be available for politicians to spend on pet projects.

These two policies could be put in place in conjunction with eliminating burdensome existing laws and regulations and using the marketplace rather than edicts by the government to do this or not do that. Put a price out there, and let the marketplace adapt. You would be surprised at its creativity.

So that is my proposal. Before you get mugged by reality, take out an insurance policy. It's the Reagan way.

A CONSERVATIVE ANSWER TO CLIMATE CHANGE

George P. Shultz and James A. Baker III

Originally published in the Wall Street Journal *on February 7, 2017. Mr. Baker was secretary of state (1989–92) and treasury secretary (1985–88).*

Thirty years ago, as the atmosphere's protective ozone layer was dwindling at alarming rates, we were serving proudly under President Ronald Reagan. We remember his leading role in negotiating the Montreal Protocol, which continues to protect and restore the delicate ozone layer. Today the world faces a similar challenge: the threat of climate change.

Just as in the 1980s, there is mounting evidence of problems with the atmosphere that are growing too compelling to ignore. And once again, there is uncertainty about what lies ahead. The extent to which climate change is due to man-made causes can be questioned, but the risks associated with future warming are so severe that they should be hedged.

The responsible and conservative response should be to take out an insurance policy. Doing so need not rely on heavy-handed, growth-inhibiting government regulations. Instead, a climate solution should be based on a sound economic analysis that embodies the conservative principles of free markets and limited government.

We suggest a solution that rests on four pillars. First, creating a gradually increasing carbon tax. Second, returning the tax proceeds to the American people in the form of dividends. Third, establishing border carbon adjustments that protect American competitiveness and encourage other countries to follow suit. And fourth, rolling back government regulations once such a system is in place.

The first pillar, a carbon tax, is the most cost-effective way to reduce emissions. Unlike the current cumbersome regulatory approach, a levy on emissions would free companies to find the most efficient way to reduce their carbon footprint. A sensibly priced, gradually rising tax would send a powerful market signal to businesses that want certainty when planning for the future.

A "carbon dividend" payment, the second pillar, would have tax proceeds distributed to the American people on a quarterly basis. This way, the revenue-neutral tax would benefit working families rather than bloating government spending. A $40-per-ton carbon tax would provide a family of four with roughly $2,000 in carbon dividends in the first year, an amount that could grow over time as the carbon tax rate increased.

A carbon dividends policy could spur reductions in greenhouse-gas emissions larger than all of President Obama's climate policies. At the same time, our plan would strengthen the economy, help working-class Americans, and promote national security, all while reducing regulations and shrinking the size of government.

The third pillar is a border adjustment for carbon content. When American companies export to countries without comparable carbon pricing systems, they would receive rebates on the carbon taxes they have paid. Imports from such countries, meanwhile, would face fees on the carbon content of their products. Proceeds from such fees would also be returned to the American people through carbon dividends. Pioneering such a system would put America in the driver's seat of global climate policy. It would also promote American competitiveness by penalizing countries whose lack of carbon-reduction policies would otherwise give them an unfair trade advantage.

The eventual elimination of regulations no longer necessary after the enactment of a carbon tax would constitute the final pillar. Almost all of the Environmental Protection Agency's regulatory authority over carbon emissions could be eliminated, including an outright repeal of President Obama's Clean Power Plan. Robust carbon taxes would also justify ending federal and state tort liability for emitters.

With these principles in mind, on Wednesday the Climate Leadership Council is unveiling "The Conservative Case for Carbon Dividends." The report was coauthored by conservative thinkers Martin Feldstein, Henry Paulson Jr., Gregory Mankiw, Ted Halstead, Tom Stephenson, and Rob Walton.

This carbon dividends program would help steer the United States toward a path of more durable economic growth by encouraging technological innovation and large-scale substitution of existing energy sources. It would also provide much-needed regulatory relief to US industries. Companies, especially those in the energy sector, finally would have the predictability they now lack, removing one of the most serious impediments to capital investment.

Perhaps most important, the carbon-dividends plan speaks to the increasing frustration and economic insecurity experienced by many working-class Americans. The plan would elevate the fortunes of the nation's less advantaged while strengthening the economy. A Treasury Department report published last month predicts that carbon dividends would mean income gains for about 70 percent of Americans.

This plan will also be good for the long-term prospects of the Republican Party. About two-thirds of Americans worry a "great deal" or "fair amount" about climate change, according to a 2016 Gallup survey. Polls often show that concern about climate change is higher among younger voters and among Asians and Hispanics, the fastest-growing demographic groups. A carbon-dividends plan provides an opportunity to appeal to all three demographics.

Controlling the White House and Congress means that Republicans bear the responsibility of exercising wise leadership on the defining challenges of our era. Climate change is one of these issues. It is time for the Grand Old Party to once again lead the way.

CHAPTER 9

Nuclear Security, Past and Future

On August 6, 1945, I was a captain in the US Marines on a troop ship bound for San Diego, where we were expecting to be formed into troops that would assault the Japanese mainland. Every Marine aboard had already experienced at least one landing—so we knew what we were headed for.

Early in the voyage we heard that something called an atomic bomb had been dropped on Hiroshima. We knew it was important, but none of us had any clue what such a thing really was. By the time the ship reached port, a second bomb had been dropped on Nagasaki, and we got the news that we would not be deployed to the Japanese mainland after all. The war was over.

Though people still didn't fully understand them, one could start to appreciate the sheer power of these weapons. In the months that followed, as a graduate student at MIT, I went to any open physics session I could to try to learn more. We were still doing atmospheric testing then, which is incredible to think about! The casinos in Las Vegas advertised nuclear getaways where tourists could book hotel rooms that faced the desert spectacle. The awesome power we were dealing with was apparent to everyone.

Years later, I vividly recall my first meeting with Gorbachev after the Chernobyl power plant accident. I learned that he had asked his military leaders the same question I had asked

Secretary of State George Shultz and wife O'Bie leaving the State Department, January 19, 1989.
COURTESY HOOVER INSTITUTION LIBRARY & ARCHIVES.

US officials, and we both were told that if it had instead been a nuclear weapon detonated at Chernobyl, the results would have been far more devastating. There was a visceral as well as intellectual realization that the power of nuclear weapons is truly awesome.

The latter part of the 1980s saw dramatic changes in the threat posed by nuclear weapons. The phrase "A nuclear war cannot be won and must never be fought," contained in one of President Reagan's State of the Union addresses, was enunciated again in 1985 at the Geneva Summit between Reagan and Gorbachev. There was a recognition of the devastating power of nuclear weapons and a desire, highlighted by Reagan's proposal in the nuclear negotiations in Geneva, to eliminate intermediate-range nuclear weapons and to cut in half the number of strategic weapons.

Today, with the Cold War over, awareness of the awesome power of nuclear weapons seems to have dissipated, but the threat remains. We are now increasingly aware of their proliferation and the increased likelihood that nuclear weapons could be used by states or even by terrorists. Following developments in Iran, the broader Middle East may now be ripe for proliferation. For example, Saudi Arabia may try to purchase weapons from Pakistan to keep parity. Meanwhile, Pakistan and India continue to build up their stockpiles of nuclear weapons, and regional tensions, such as those surrounding Kashmir, continue unabated. Then there is North Korea.

But it is the Russians with whom we need first engage. As I spelled out in the introduction to this book, I think there is a chance of finding some common ground from which to pursue this. The idea that we "ought" to work toward a world free of nuclear weapons is still shared in both countries, just as it was in the closing years of the Cold War. But the path to doing so still isn't obvious. If we wish to develop the conditions for a constructive dialogue, it is important that we place that goal within an updated framework for understanding Russian interests and Russian fears. That is what I set out to do in my 1983 Senate testimony, early in my posting as secretary of state. It is a framework for approaching US-Soviet relations from a position of strength and without rose-tinted glasses. And it is worth revisiting today.

Meanwhile, we should aim to reawaken consciousness of the power of nuclear weapons among ordinary people to enlist their support in developing a more constructive atmosphere for dealing with them. As my friend Bill Swing, the retired Episcopal bishop of California, once observed, the US president may put his hand on the Bible at his inauguration, but it is when he puts his hand on the nuclear trigger that "you will be like God." Bishop Swing's thoughts on this issue are included at the conclusion of this book.

People may be vaguely aware that if a nuclear weapon hits their city, the city will disappear, as if smitten by God. Immediate deaths in Hiroshima were nearly 150,000. A single "low-yield" groundburst of that same size—fifteen kilotons— in today's dense megacities would be even worse. A regional nuclear war would be more deadly, of course: a confrontation between India and Pakistan would result in ten million immediate casualties. In 2007 a professor named Owen Toon from the University of Colorado estimated that just three Hiroshima-size blasts in the United States, concentrated on New York City, would exceed all American deaths during the Second World War.[11]

Interestingly, modern atmospheric models actually give us the chance to take another look at the global effects of even a "limited" regional nuclear war in ways we never could during the Cold War. They show that what happens in one part of the world could have ramifications far beyond. For example, airbursts from a nuclear exchange between India and Pakistan could trigger widespread urban fires. As cities burned, they would produce huge amounts of soot. The soot, heated by the sun like discharge from a volcano, could spread around the globe and remain in the air for a decade, high enough for rainfall not to affect it. Ozone losses would drive up skin cancer risk. Meanwhile, average global temperatures could rapidly fall by two to three degrees Fahrenheit, worse in some places than in others, and stay that way for decades. And the world would get drier, with rainfall in Asia reduced by up to half.

Farming would take the brunt of all of this: Chinese rice production levels might fall by one-fifth, sending them back to supply levels of the early 1990s. What upheavals might result? Frost could persist for an extra month each year, resulting in fewer and shorter growing seasons. And global fisheries would be affected by rapid cooling of the upper ocean. The results could disrupt global human health, food production, and other ecosystems for years. This from an arsenal representing less than 0.1 percent of today's global nuclear weapons yield.[12]

I don't dwell on this topic to scare people, but I do aim to get it into their gut. We desperately need a new effort to make everyone understand the power of nuclear weapons and the implications of careless attitudes toward their use. Any use of nuclear weapons, anywhere, would have consequences for us all. Albert Einstein observed that "the unleashed power of the atom has changed everything except our thinking. . . . We shall require a substantially new manner of thinking if mankind is to survive." We have to remind ourselves that, still today, whether we dwell on it or not, we are as much like God as we are men.

I conclude on this topic, and the essays here document my approach to dealing with nuclear weapons from the Reagan administration through today. I hope that we can keep this on the minds of the next generation as they, too, think about the future.

US-SOVIET RELATIONS IN THE CONTEXT
OF US FOREIGN POLICY

Statement by Secretary of State George P. Shultz before the Senate Foreign Relations Committee, June 15, 1983.

I appreciate the opportunity to meet with you and to discuss this subject of great importance. As you have suggested, it has all sorts of dimensions to it that weigh on people's minds; it is a subject that I've thought about a great deal, of course. The president has. You might say that the president has not only taken the time to talk with me about this, but has read through this testimony and made a few suggestions, which I found it possible to accept, and has signed off on the testimony. So I feel very confident in saying that I am speaking not only for myself but for the president in this statement.

The management of our relations with the Soviet Union is of utmost importance. That relationship touches virtually every aspect of our international concerns and objectives—political, economic, and military—and every part of the world.

We must defend our interests and values against a powerful Soviet adversary that threatens both. And we must do so in a nuclear age, in which a global war would even more thoroughly threaten those interests and values. As President Reagan pointed out on March 31, "We must both defend freedom and preserve the peace. We must stand true to our principles and our friends while preventing a holocaust." It is, as he said, "one of the most complex moral challenges ever faced by any generation."

We and the Soviets have sharply divergent goals and philosophies of political and moral order; these differences will not soon go away. Any other assumption is unrealistic. At the same time, we have a fundamental common interest in the avoidance of war. This common interest impels us to work toward a relationship between our nations that can lead to a safer world for all mankind.

But a safer world will not be realized through goodwill. Our hopes for the future must be grounded in a realistic assessment of the challenges we face and in a determined effort to create the conditions that will make their achievement possible. We have made a start. Every postwar American president has come sooner or later to recognize that peace must be built on strength; President Reagan has long recognized this reality. In the past two years, this nation—the president in partnership with the Congress—has made a fundamental commitment to restoring its military and economic power, and moral and spiritual strength. And having begun to rebuild our strength, we now seek to engage the Soviet leaders in a constructive dialogue—a dialogue through which we hope to find political solutions to outstanding issues.

This is the central goal we have pursued since the outset of this administration. We do not want to—and need not—accept as inevitable the prospect of endless, dangerous confrontation with the Soviet Union. For if we do, then many of the great goals that the United States pursues in world affairs—peace, human rights, economic progress, national independence—will also be out of reach. We can—and must—do better.

With that introduction, let me briefly lay out for this committee what I see as the challenge posed by the Soviet Union's international behavior in recent years and the strategy that challenge requires of us. Then I would like to discuss steps this administration has taken to implement that strategy. Finally, I will focus on the specific issues that make up the agenda for US-Soviet dialogue and negotiation.

Together, these elements constitute a policy that takes account of the facts of Soviet power and of Soviet conduct, mobilizes the resources needed to defend our interests, and offers an agenda for constructive dialogue to resolve concrete international problems. We believe that, if sustained, this policy will make international restraint Moscow's most realistic course, and it can lay the foundation for a more constructive relationship between our peoples.

The Soviet Challenge

It is sometimes said that Americans have too simple a view of world affairs, that we start with the assumption that all problems can be solved. Certainly we have a simple view of how the world should be: free peoples choosing their own destinies, nurturing their prosperity, peaceably resolving conflicts. This is the vision that inspires America's role in the world. It does not, however, lead us to regard mutual hostility with the USSR as an immutable fact of international life.

Certainly there are many factors contributing to East-West tension. The Soviet Union's strategic Eurasian location places it in close proximity to important Western interests on two continents. Its aspirations for greater international influence lead it to challenge these interests. Its Marxist-Leninist ideology gives its leaders a perspective on history and a vision of the future fundamentally different from our own. But we are not so deterministic as to believe that geopolitics and ideological competition must ineluctably lead to permanent and dangerous confrontation. Nor is it permanently inevitable that contention between the United States and the Soviet Union must dominate and distort international politics.

A peaceful world order does not require that we and the Soviet Union agree on all the fundamentals of morals or politics. It does require, however, that Moscow's behavior be subject to the restraint appropriate to living together on this planet in the nuclear age. Not all the many external and internal factors affecting Soviet behavior can be influenced by us. But we take it as part of our obligation to peace to encourage the gradual evolution of the Soviet system toward a more pluralistic political and economic system and, above all, to counter Soviet expansionism through sustained and effective political, economic, and military competition.

In the past decade, regrettably, the changes in Soviet behavior have been for the worse. Soviet actions have come into conflict with many of our objectives. They have made the task of managing the Soviet-American relationship considerably harder and have needlessly drawn more and more international problems into the East-West rivalry. To be specific, the following developments have caused us the most concern.

First is the continuing Soviet quest for military superiority even in the face of mounting domestic economic difficulties. In the late 1970s the allocation of resources for the Soviet military was not only at the expense of the Soviet consumer. It came even at the expense of industrial investment on which the long-term development of the economy depends. This decision to mortgage the industrial future of the country is a striking demonstration of the inordinate value the Soviets assign to maintaining the momentum of the relentless military buildup under way since the mid-1960s. This buildup consumed an estimated annual average of at least 12 percent of the Soviet gross national product (GNP) throughout this entire period and has recently consumed even more as a result of the sharp decline in Soviet economic growth. During much of this same period, as you know, the share of our own GNP devoted to defense spending has actually declined.

The second disturbing development is the unconstructive Soviet involvement, direct and indirect, in unstable areas of the Third World. Arms have become a larger percentage of Soviet exports than of the export trade of any other country. The Soviets have too often attempted to play a spoiling or scavenging role in areas of concern to us, most recently in the Middle East.

Beyond this, the Soviets in the 1970s broke major new ground in the kinds of foreign military intervention they were willing to risk for themselves or their surrogates. This has escalated from the provision of large numbers of military advisers to the more extensive and aggressive use of proxy forces, as in Angola, Ethiopia, and Indochina, and finally to the massive employment of the Soviet Union's own ground troops in the invasion of Afghanistan. In this way, the Soviet Union has tried to block peaceful solutions and has brought East-West tensions into areas of the world that were once free of them.

Third is the unrelenting effort to impose an alien Soviet "model" on nominally independent Soviet clients and allies. One of the most important recent achievements in East-West relations was the negotiation of the Helsinki Final Act, with its pledges concerning human rights and national independence in Europe. Poland's experience in the past two years can be considered a major test of the Soviet Union's respect—or lack of it—for these commitments. Moscow clearly remains unwilling to countenance meaningful national autonomy for its satellites, let alone real independence. Elsewhere in the world, the coming to power of Soviet-supported regimes has usually meant (as in Afghanistan) forcible creation of Soviet-style institutions and harsh regimentation and repression of free expression and free initiative—all at enormous human, cultural, and economic cost.

Fourth is Moscow's continuing practice of stretching a series of treaties and agreements to the brink of violation and beyond. The Soviet Union's infringement of its promises and legal obligations is not confined to isolated incidents. We have had to express our concerns about Soviet infractions on one issue after another—human rights and the Helsinki Final Act, "yellow rain" and biological warfare. We are becoming increasingly concerned about Soviet practices—including the recent testing of ICBMs [intercontinental ballistic missiles]—that raise questions about the validity of their claim of compliance with existing SALT [strategic arms limitation talks] agreements. Little else is so corrosive of international trust as this persistent pattern of Soviet behavior.

The American Response: Beyond Containment and Detente

This assessment of Soviet international behavior both dictates the approach we must take to East-West relations and indicates the magnitude of the task.

- If we are concerned about the Soviet commitment to military power, we have to take steps *to restore the military balance*, preferably on the basis of verifiable agreements that reduce arms on both sides but, if necessary, through our own and allied defense programs.
- If we are concerned about the Soviet propensity to use force and promote instability, we have to make clear that we will *resist encroachments* on our vital interests and those of our allies and friends.
- If we are concerned about the loss of liberty that results when Soviet clients come to power, then we have to

ensure that those who have a positive alternative to the Soviet model receive our support.

- Finally, if we are concerned about Moscow's observance of its international obligations, we must *leave Moscow no opportunity to distort or misconstrue our own intentions.* We will defend our interests if Soviet conduct leaves us no alternative; at the same time we will respect legitimate Soviet security interests and are ready to negotiate equitable solutions to outstanding political problems.

In designing a strategy to meet these goals, we have, of course, drawn in part on past strategies, from containment to detente. There is, after all, substantial continuity in US policy, a continuity that reflects the consistency of American values and American interests. However, we have not hesitated to jettison assumptions about US-Soviet relations that have been refuted by experience or overtaken by events.

Consider how the world has changed since the Truman administration developed the doctrine of containment. Soviet ambitions and capabilities have long since reached beyond the geographic bounds that this doctrine took for granted. Today Moscow conducts a fully global foreign and military policy that places global demands on any strategy that aims to counter it. Where it was once our goal to contain the Soviet presence within the limits of its immediate postwar reach, now our goal must be to advance our own objectives, where possible foreclosing and when necessary actively countering Soviet challenges wherever they threaten our interests.

The policy of detente, of course, represented an effort to induce Soviet restraint. While in some versions it recognized the need to resist Soviet geopolitical encroachments, it also hoped that the anticipation of benefits from expanding economic relations and arms control agreements would restrain Soviet behavior.

Unfortunately, experience has proved otherwise. The economic relationship may have eased some of the domestic Soviet economic constraints that might have at least marginally inhibited Moscow's behavior. It also raised the specter of a future Western dependence on Soviet bloc trade that would inhibit Western freedom of action toward the East more than it would dictate prudence to the USSR. Similarly, the SALT I and SALT II processes did not curb the Soviet strategic arms buildup, while encouraging many in the West to imagine that security concerns could now be placed lower on the agenda.

Given these differences from the past, we have not been able merely to tinker with earlier approaches. Unlike containment, our policy begins with the clear recognition that the Soviet Union is and will remain a global superpower. In response to the lessons of this global superpower's conduct in recent years, our policy, unlike some versions of detente, assumes that the Soviet Union is more likely to be deterred by actions that make clear the risks entailed by their aggression than by a delicate web of interdependence.

Our policy is not based on trust or on a Soviet change of heart. It is based on the expectation that, faced with a demonstration of the West's renewed determination to strengthen its defenses, enhance its political and economic cohesion, and oppose adventurism, the Soviet Union will see restraint as its most attractive, or only, option. Perhaps, over time, this restraint will become an ingrained habit; perhaps not. Either way, our responsibility to be vigilant is the same.

Programs to Increase Our Strength

In a rapidly evolving international environment, there are many fundamental ways the democratic nations can, and must, advance their own goals in the face of the problem posed by the Soviet Union. We must build a durable political consensus at home and within the Atlantic alliance on the nature of the Soviet challenge. We must strengthen our defenses and those of our allies. We must build a common approach within the alliance on the strategic implications of East-West economic relations. And we must compete peacefully and even more effectively with the USSR for the political sympathies of the global electorate, especially through promotion of economic dynamism and democracy throughout the world. Finally, we must continue rebuilding America's moral-spiritual strength. If sustained over time, these policies can foster a progressively more productive dialogue with the Soviet Union itself.

Building Consensus

From the beginning of this administration, the president recognized how essential it was to consolidate a new consensus, here at home and among our traditional allies and friends. After fifteen years in which foreign policy had been an increasingly divisive issue, he believed we had an opportunity to shape a new unity in America, expressing the American people's recovery of self-confidence. After the trauma of Vietnam, he sought to bolster a realistic pride in our country and to reinforce the civic courage and commitment on which the credibility of our military deterrent ultimately rests.

The president also felt that the possibility of greater cooperation with our allies depended importantly on a reaffirmation of our common moral values and interests. There were, as well, opportunities for cooperation with friendly governments of the developing world and new efforts to seek and achieve common objectives.

Redressing the Military Balance

President Reagan also began a major effort to modernize our military forces. The central goal of our national security policy is deterrence of war; restoring and maintaining the strategic balance is a necessary condition for that deterrence. But the strategic balance also shapes, to an important degree, the global environment in which the United States pursues its foreign policy objectives. Therefore, decisions on major strategic weapons systems can have profound political as well as military consequences.

As secretary of state I am acutely conscious of the strength or weakness of American power and its effect on our influence over events. Perceptions of the strategic balance are bound to affect the judgments of not only our adversaries but also our allies and friends around the world who rely on us. As leader of the democratic nations, we have an inescapable responsibility to maintain this pillar of the military balance, which only we can maintain.

Our determination to do so is an important signal of our resolve and is essential to sustaining the confidence of allies and friends and the cohesion of our alliances. This is why the Congress's support of the Peacekeeper ICBM program has been such a valuable contribution to our foreign policy, as well as to our defense.

At the same time, we have begun an accelerated program to strengthen our conventional capabilities. We are pursuing major improvements of our ground, naval, and tactical air forces; we have also added a new Central Command in the Middle East, which will enhance our ability to deploy forces rapidly if threats to our vital interests make this necessary. To deter or deal with any future crisis, we need to maintain both our conventional capabilities and our strategic deterrent.

We are also working closely with our allies to improve our collective defense. As shown in the security declaration of the Williamsburg summit and in the North Atlantic Council communiqué of just the other day, we and our allies are united in our approach in the INF [intermediate-range nuclear forces] negotiations in Geneva and remain on schedule for the deployment of Pershing II and ground-launched cruise missiles. That deployment will take place as planned unless we are able to reach a balanced and verifiable agreement at Geneva that makes deployment unnecessary.

Upgrading NATO's conventional forces is, of course, a collective alliance responsibility. At the NATO summit in Bonn a year ago, the president and the leaders of the Atlantic alliance reaffirmed that a credible conventional defense is essential to ensuring European security. We and our allies will continue our efforts toward this goal. At the same time, we have taken steps to ensure a more equitable sharing of the burden of that defense. As a measure of the value of such steps, we estimate that the arrangement dictated in last year's agreement with the FRG [Federal Republic of Germany] on host-nation support will cost about 10 percent of what it would cost to provide the same capability with US reserves, or 3 percent of what it would cost to provide that capability with active forces.

The Soviets apparently believe they can weaken or divide the Western alliance if they can dominate outlying strategic areas and resources. To deter threats to our vital interests outside Europe, we are developing our ability to move forces, supported by our allies, to key areas of the world such as Southwest Asia. The allies are also working with us to contribute to stability and security in certain volatile areas, including Lebanon and the Sinai.

In Asia we are modernizing our forces and working with our allies, especially Japan and Korea, to improve their ability to fulfill agreed roles and missions.

Reassessing the Security Implications of East-West Economic Relations

The balance of power cannot be measured simply in terms of military forces or hardware; military power rests on a foundation of economic strength. Thus, we and our allies must not only strengthen our own economies but also develop a common approach to our economic relations with the Soviet Union that takes into account our broad strategic and security interests. In the past, the nations of the West have sometimes helped the Soviets avoid difficult economic choices by allowing them to acquire militarily relevant technology and subsidized credits. Possible dependence on energy imports from the Soviet Union is another cause for concern.

In the past year, we have made substantial progress toward an allied consensus on East-West trade. The Williamsburg summit declaration stated clearly: "East-West economic relations should be compatible with our security interests." The NATO communiqué two days ago made a similar statement. Our allies agree with us that trade which makes a clear and direct contribution to the military strength of the Soviet Union should be prohibited. There is also general agreement that economic relations with the USSR should be conducted on the basis of a strict balance of mutual advantages.

Studies undertaken under NATO and OECD [Organization for Economic Cooperation and Development] auspices have for the first time laid the groundwork for common analyses. We expect in time to draw common policy conclusions from these studies. The communiqué of the OECD ministerial meeting on May 9–10 declared that "East-West trade and credit flows should be guided by the indications of the market. In the light of these indications, Governments should exercise financial prudence without granting preferential treatment." The United States seeks agreement that we not subsidize Soviet imports through the terms of government credits. Beyond this, we urge other Western governments to exercise restraint in providing or guaranteeing credit to the Soviet Union, allowing the commercial considerations of the market to govern credit.

Similarly, at the IEA [International Energy Agency] ministerial meeting in Paris on May 8, it was agreed that security concerns should be considered among the full costs of imported energy, such as gas; it was agreed that countries "would seek to avoid undue dependence on any one source of gas imports and to obtain future gas supplies from secure sources, with emphasis on indigenous OECD sources."

The fruitful cooperative discussions of these issues at the OECD, IEA, Williamsburg, and NATO are only a beginning. Economic relationships are a permanent element of the strategic equation. How the West should respond economically to the Soviet challenge will and should be a subject of continuing discussion in Western forums for years to come.

Peace and Stability in the Third World

Since the 1950s, the Soviet Union has found in the developing regions of the Third World its greatest opportunities for extending its influence through subversion and exploitation of local conflicts. A satisfactory East-West military balance will not by itself close off such opportunities. We must also respond to the economic, political, and security problems that contribute to these opportunities. Our approach has four key elements.

First, in the many areas where Soviet activities have added to instability, we are pursuing peaceful diplomatic solutions to regional problems, to raise the political costs of Soviet-backed military presence and to encourage the departure of Soviet-backed forces. Our achievements in the Middle East, while far from complete, are addressed to this goal; we are actively encouraging

ASEAN [Association of South East Asian Nations] efforts to bring about Vietnamese withdrawal from Kampuchea; we strongly support the worldwide campaign for Soviet withdrawal from Afghanistan; and we have made considerable progress toward an internationally acceptable agreement on Namibia. In our own hemisphere, we are working with other regional states in support of a peaceful solution to the conflict and instability in Central America.

Second, we are building up the security capabilities of vulnerable governments in strategically important areas. We are helping our friends to help themselves and to help each other. For this purpose, we are asking the Congress for a larger, more flexible security assistance program for FY 1984.

Third, our program recognizes that economic crisis and political instability create fertile ground for Soviet-sponsored adventurism. We are seeking almost $4 billion in economic assistance to help developing countries lay the basis for economic and social progress. We are seeking congressional approval to raise IMF [International Monetary Fund] quotas and broaden IMF borrowing arrangements to address critical financial needs of some of the largest Third World nations. We urge the Congress to approve the full amount requested by the administration toward meeting the US commitment to the IDA [International Development Association].

Finally, there is the democracy initiative, an effort to assist our friends in the Third World to build a foundation for democracy. I might say it has been fascinating to me, as this project, which is very small, has gotten started, to see the reaction to it. We held a meeting in the State Department with people from various parts of the world on the subject of free elections, and it was denounced by the Soviet Union. The interesting thing was, they noticed it. I was struck by the fact that in Mr. Chernenko's [Communist Party secretary] speech yesterday one of the subjects he brought out was the importance to them of destroying President Reagan's, in a sense, ideological initiatives. It seems we have their attention. And I think if we actually can frame competition on the basis of ideologies, on the basis of economic systems, then we'll walk away with it.

Negotiation and Dialogue: The US-Soviet Agenda

Together these programs increase our political, military, and economic strength and help create an international climate in which opportunities for Soviet adventurism are reduced. They are essential for the success of the final element of our strategy: engaging the Soviets in an active and productive dialogue on the concrete issues that concern the two sides. Strength and realism can deter war, but only direct dialogue and negotiation can open the path toward lasting peace. In this dialogue, our agenda is as follows:

- to seek improvement in Soviet performance on human rights;
- to reduce the risk of war, reduce armaments through sound agreements, and ultimately ease the burdens of military spending;
- to manage and resolve regional conflicts; and
- to improve bilateral relations on the basis of reciprocity and mutual interest.

This is a rigorous and comprehensive agenda, and our approach to it is principled, practical, and patient. We have pressed each issue in a variety of forums, bilateral and multilateral. We have made clear that the concerns we raise are not ours alone, but are shared by our allies and friends in every region of the globe. We have made clear that each of our concerns is serious, and the Soviets know that we do not intend to abandon any of them merely because agreement cannot be reached quickly or because agreement has been reached on others.

Let me briefly review the state of our dialogue in each of these areas.

Human Rights

Human rights is a major issue on our agenda. To us it is a matter of real concern that Soviet emigration is at its lowest level since the

1960s and that Soviet constriction of emigration has coincided with a general crackdown against all forms of internal dissent. The Helsinki monitoring groups have all been dispersed, and their leaders have been imprisoned or expelled from the country. And the Soviet Union's first independent disarmament group has been harassed and persecuted.

We address such questions both multilaterally and bilaterally. In such forums as the UN Human Rights Commission, the International Labor Organization, and especially the review conference of CSCE [Conference on Security and Cooperation in Europe]—I might say where Max Kampelman [chairman of the US delegation] is doing an absolutely outstanding job—we have made clear that human rights cannot be relegated to the margins of international politics. Our Soviet interlocutors have a different view; they seek to dismiss human rights as a "tenth-rate issue," not worthy of high-level attention.

But our approach will not change. Americans know that national rights and individual rights cannot realistically be kept separate. We believe, for example, that the elements of the postwar European "settlement" that were adopted by the parties to the Helsinki Final Act in 1975 form an integral whole; no one part will survive alone. Guided by this conviction, we and our allies have held at the Madrid review conference that movement in one "basket" of this settlement—such as the convening of a European disarmament conference—must be matched by progress in the other "baskets," especially human rights.

We insist on this balance because we believe that international obligations must be taken seriously by the governments that assume them. But there is also a deeper reason that directly concerns the question of security. In Europe, as elsewhere, governments that are not at peace with their own people are unlikely to be on good terms with their neighbors. The only significant use of military force on the continent of Europe since 1945 has been by the Soviet Union against its East European "allies." As long as this unnatural relationship continues between the USSR and its East European neighbors, it is bound to be a source of instability in Europe.

We have been just as concerned about human rights issues on a bilateral as on a multilateral basis. The need for steady improvement of Soviet performance in the most important human rights categories is as central to the Soviet-American dialogue as any other theme. Sometimes we advance this dialogue best through public expressions of our concerns, at other times through quiet diplomacy. What counts, and the Soviets know this, is whether we see results.

Arms Control

Let me turn to arms control. We believe the only arms control agreements that count are those that provide for real reductions, equality, verifiability, and enhanced stability in the East-West balance. Success in our negotiations will not, of course, bring East-West competition to an end. But sustainable agreements will enable us to meet the Soviet challenge in a setting of greater stability and safety.

The United States is now applying these principles in an ambitious program of arms control negotiations, including INF, START [strategic arms reduction talks], MBFR [mutual and balanced force reductions], and the ongoing discussions in the UN Committee on Disarmament in Geneva. If we can reach a balanced agreement in the CSCE at Madrid, we would be prepared to participate also in a conference on disarmament in Europe.

No previous administration has put so many elements of the East-West military equation on the negotiating table. You are aware of the US position in the various talks, so I need not go into great detail. I will, however, touch on a few main points.

START. In the strategic arms reduction talks the United States has focused on the most destabilizing strategic systems: land-based ballistic missiles. Our objective is to strengthen deterrence while enhancing strategic stability through reductions. The president has proposed reducing ballistic missile warheads by one-third. In presenting a comprehensive proposal, he has indicated that all strategic weapons are on the table. Although our respective positions are far apart, the Soviets apparently accept the proposition that an agreement must involve significant reductions. This is progress.

We have recently undertaken a full review of the US position, which included an assessment of the Scowcroft commission's recommendations and some thoughtful suggestions from the Congress. One week ago, the president announced that he is willing to raise the deployed-missile ceiling in accordance with the Scowcroft recommendations. He also announced that he has given our negotiators new flexibility to explore all appropriate avenues for achieving reductions. It is now up to the Soviet Union to reciprocate our flexibility.

Confidence-Building Measures. We have also tabled a draft agreement on confidence-building measures that calls for exchange of information and advance notification of ballistic missile launches and major exercises. We want to move forward promptly to negotiate separate agreements on these very important measures, which would enhance stability in a crisis as well as symbolizing the common interest in preventing war. Yet another effort to prevent misperception of military activities on either side, and thus to lower the risk of war, is the president's recent proposal to expand and upgrade crisis communications between Washington and Moscow. Here, too, we hope for early agreement.

INF. In the negotiations on intermediate-range nuclear forces, "equal rights and limits" between the United States and the Soviet Union is one of our key principles. President Reagan's proposal of November 1981 sought to achieve the complete elimination of those systems on each side about which the other side has expressed the greatest concern—that is, longer-range, land-based INF missiles.

We still regard this as the most desirable outcome. Yet after more than a year of talks, the Soviets continue to resist this equitable and effective solution. In fact, their position has not substantially changed since it was first put forward nearly a year ago. The proposal made by Mr. Andropov [general secretary of the Communist Party] last December would allow the Soviet Union to maintain its overwhelming monopoly of longer-range INF (LRINF) missiles while prohibiting the deployment of even one comparable US missile.

In an effort to break this stalemate, the president has proposed an interim agreement as a route to the eventual elimination of LRINF systems. Under such an agreement, we would reduce the number of missiles we plan to deploy in Europe if the Soviet Union will reduce the total number of warheads it has already deployed to an equal level. This would result in equal limits for both sides on a global basis. Reflecting the concerns of our Asian allies and friends, we have made it clear that no agreement can come at their expense. We hope that in the current round of negotiations the Soviets will move to negotiate in good faith on the president's proposal, which was unanimously supported by our partners at the Williamsburg summit.

MBFR. In the mutual and balanced force reductions talks in Vienna, NATO and the Warsaw Pact are discussing an agreement on conventional forces in Central Europe, the most heavily armed region of the world, where Warsaw Pact forces greatly exceed NATO's. Last year, the president announced a new Western position in the form of a draft treaty calling for substantial reductions to equal manpower levels. Although the Soviets and their allies have agreed to the principle of parity, progress has been prevented by inability to resolve disagreement over existing Warsaw Pact force levels and by problems of verification.

Chemical Weapons. In the forty-nation Committee on Disarmament in Geneva, the United States has introduced a far-reaching proposal for a comprehensive ban on chemical weapons—an agreement that would eliminate these terrible weapons from world arsenals. This initiative has been vigorously supported by our allies and friends, as well as by many nonaligned nations. Our emphasis on the importance of mandatory on-site inspections has been widely applauded. An independent, impartial verification system, observed by and responsive to all parties, is essential to create confidence that the ban is being respected.

Nuclear Testing and Nonproliferation. In other areas, we have proposed to the Soviet Union improvements in the verification provisions of two agreements to limit underground nuclear testing. So far the Soviet response has been negative. We have also initiated a dialogue with the Soviets in one area where our respective approaches very often coincide: nuclear nonproliferation. We should not anticipate early agreement in any of these negotiations. The Soviets have their own positions, and they are tough, patient negotiators. But we believe that our positions are fair and evenhanded and that our objectives are realistic.

Regional Issues

Let me now turn to regional issues, which in the sweep of things historically have been the matters that are most upsetting to our relationship with the Soviet Union. Important as it is, arms control has not been—and cannot be—the dominant subject of our dialogue with the Soviets. We must also address the threat to peace posed by the Soviet exploitation of regional instability and conflict. Indeed, these issues—arms control and political instability—are closely related: the increased stability that we try to build into the superpower relationship through arms control can be undone by irresponsible Soviet policies elsewhere. In our numerous discussions with the Soviet leadership, we have repeatedly expressed our strong interest in reaching understandings with the Soviets that would minimize superpower involvement in conflicts beyond their borders.

The list of problem areas is formidable, but we have insisted that regional issues are central to progress. We have made clear our commitment to relieve repression and economic distress in Poland, to achieve a settlement in southern Africa, to restore independence to Afghanistan, to end the occupation of Kampuchea, and to halt Soviet- and Cuban-supported subversion in Central America. In each instance, we have conveyed our views forcefully to the Soviets in an attempt to remove the obstacles that Soviet conduct puts in the way of resolving these problems.

Last year, for example, Ambassador Hartman [US ambassador to the USSR] conducted a round of exploratory talks on Afghanistan between US and Soviet officials in Moscow. Any solution to the Afghanistan problem must meet four requirements: complete withdrawal of Soviet forces, restoration of Afghanistan's independent and nonaligned status, formation of a government acceptable to the Afghan people, and honorable return of the refugees. This is not the view of the United States alone. These principles underlie the discussions now under way under the auspices of the UN secretary general, which we support.

On southern African problems, Assistant Secretary Crocker has held a number of detailed exchanges with his Soviet counterpart. Southern Africa has been a point of tension and periodic friction between the United States and the Soviet Union for many years. We want to see tensions in the area reduced. But this more peaceful future will not be achieved unless all parties interested in the region show restraint, external military forces are withdrawn, and Namibia is permitted to achieve independence. If the Soviets are at all concerned with the interests of Africans, they should have an equal interest in achieving these objectives.

As in our arms control negotiations, we have made it absolutely clear to the Soviets in these discussions that we are not interested in cosmetic solutions. We are interested in solving problems fundamental to maintenance of the international order.

It is also our view that Soviet participation in international efforts to resolve regional conflicts—in southern Africa or the Middle East, for example—depends on Soviet conduct. If the Soviets seek to benefit from tension and support those who promote disorder, they can hardly expect to have a role in the amelioration of those problems. Nor should we expect them to act responsibly merely because they gain a role. At the same time, we have also made it clear that we will not exploit and, in fact, are prepared to respond positively to Soviet restraint. The decision in each case is theirs.

Bilateral Relations

The final part of our agenda with the Soviets comprises economic and other bilateral relations. In our dialogue, we have spelled out our view of these matters in a candid and forthright way. As we see it, economic transactions can confer important strategic benefits, and we must be mindful of the implications for our security. Therefore, as I have already indicated, we believe economic relations with the East deserve more careful scrutiny than in the past. But our policy is not one of economic warfare against the USSR. East-West trade in nonstrategic areas—in the words of the NATO communiqué—"conducted on the basis of commercially sound terms and mutual advantage, that avoids preferential treatment of the Soviet Union, contributes to constructive East-West relations."

Despite the strains of the past few years in our overall relationship, we have maintained the key elements in the structure for bilateral trade. We have recently agreed with the USSR to extend our bilateral fisheries agreement for one year and have begun to negotiate a new long-term US-Soviet grain agreement. Our grain sales are on commercial terms and are not made with government-supported credits or guarantees of any kind.

As for contacts between people, we have cut back on largely symbolic exchanges but maintained a framework of cooperation in scientific, technical, and humanitarian fields. A major consideration as we pursue such exchanges must be reciprocity. If the Soviet Union is to enjoy virtually unlimited opportunities for access to our free society, US access to Soviet society must increase. We have made progress toward gaining Soviet acceptance of this principle, as indicated by the airing in Moscow this past weekend of an interview with Deputy Secretary Ken Dam.

Eight bilateral cooperative agreements are now in effect, and exchanges between the Academies of Science continue, as do exchanges of young scholars and Fulbright fellows. *America Illustrated* magazine continues to be distributed in the Soviet Union in return for distribution here of *Soviet Life*, in spite of the absence of a cultural exchanges agreement. Toward the private sector we have maintained an attitude of neither encouraging nor discouraging exchanges, and a steady flow of tourists and conference participants goes on in both directions. The number of US news bureaus in Moscow has actually increased in the last year.

Prospects

Let me just say a word about prospects. It is sometimes said that Soviet-American relations are "worse than ever." This committee's staff, for example, has made such a judgment in a recent report. Certainly the issues dividing our two countries are serious. But let us not be misled by "atmospherics," whether sunny or, as they now seem to be, stormy.

In the mid-1950s, for example, despite the rhetoric and tension of the Cold War—and in the midst of a leadership transition—the Soviet Union chose to conclude the Austrian State Treaty. It was an important agreement, which contributed to the security of Central Europe, and it carries an important lesson for us today. The Soviet leadership did not negotiate seriously merely because Western rhetoric was firm and principled, nor should we expect rhetoric to suffice now or in the future. But adverse "atmospherics" did not prevent agreement; Soviet policy was instead affected by the pattern of Western actions, by our resolve and clarity of purpose. And the result was progress.

There is no certainty that our current negotiations with the Soviets will lead to acceptable agreements. What is certain is that we will not find ourselves in the position in which we found ourselves in the aftermath of detente. We have not staked so much on the prospect of a successful negotiating outcome that we have neglected to secure ourselves against the possibility of failure. Unlike the immediate postwar period, when negotiating progress was a remote prospect, we attach the highest importance to articulating the requirements for an improved relationship and to exploring every serious avenue for progress. Our parallel pursuit of strength and negotiation prepares us both to resist continued Soviet aggrandizement and to recognize and respond to positive Soviet moves.

We have spelled out our requirements—and our hope—for a more constructive relationship with the Soviet Union. The direction in which that relationship evolves will ultimately be determined by the decisions of the Soviet leadership. President Brezhnev's successors will have to weigh the increased costs and risks of relentless competition against the benefits of a less tense international environment in which they could more adequately address the rising expectations of their own citizens. While we can define their alternatives, we cannot decipher their intentions. To a degree unequaled anywhere else, Russia in this respect remains a secret.

Its history, of which this secrecy is such an integral part, provides no basis for expecting a dramatic change. And yet it also teaches that gradual change is possible. For our part, we seek to encourage change by a firm but flexible US strategy, resting on a broad consensus, that we can sustain over the long term whether the Soviet Union changes or not. If the democracies can meet this challenge, they can achieve the goals of which President Reagan spoke at Los Angeles: both defend freedom and preserve the peace.

A WORLD FREE OF NUCLEAR WEAPONS

George P. Shultz, William J. Perry,
Henry A. Kissinger, and Sam Nunn

Originally published in the Wall Street Journal *on January 4, 2007. Mr. Perry was secretary of defense from 1994 to 1997. Mr. Kissinger, chairman of Kissinger Associates, was secretary of state from 1973 to 1977. Mr. Nunn is former chairman of the Senate Armed Services Committee.*

Nuclear weapons today present tremendous dangers but also a historic opportunity. US leadership will be required to take the world to the next stage—to a solid consensus for reversing reliance on nuclear weapons globally as a vital contribution to preventing their proliferation into potentially dangerous hands and ultimately ending them as a threat to the world.

Nuclear weapons were essential to maintaining international security during the Cold War because they were a means of deterrence. The end of the Cold War made the doctrine of mutual Soviet-American deterrence obsolete. Deterrence continues to be a relevant consideration for many states with regard to threats from other states. But reliance on nuclear weapons for this purpose is becoming increasingly hazardous and decreasingly effective.

North Korea's recent nuclear test and Iran's refusal to stop its program to enrich uranium—potentially to weapons grade—highlight the fact that the world is now on the precipice of a new and dangerous nuclear era. Most alarmingly, the likelihood that nonstate terrorists will get their hands on nuclear weaponry is increasing. In today's war waged on world order by terrorists, nuclear weapons are the ultimate means of mass devastation. And nonstate terrorist groups with nuclear weapons are conceptually outside the bounds of a deterrent strategy and present difficult new security challenges.

Apart from the terrorist threat, unless urgent new actions are taken, the United States soon will be compelled to enter a new nuclear era that will be more precarious, psychologically disorienting, and economically even more costly than was Cold War deterrence. It is far from certain that we can successfully replicate the old Soviet-American "mutually assured destruction" with an increasing number of potential nuclear enemies worldwide without dramatically increasing the risk that nuclear weapons will be used. New nuclear states do not have the benefit of years of step-by-step safeguards put in effect during the Cold War to prevent nuclear accidents, misjudgments, or unauthorized launches. The United States and the Soviet Union learned from mistakes that were less than fatal. Both countries were diligent in ensuring that no nuclear weapon was used during the Cold War by design or by accident. Will new nuclear nations and the world be as fortunate in the next fifty years as we were during the Cold War?

* * *

Leaders addressed this issue in earlier times. In his "Atoms for Peace" address to the United Nations in 1953, Dwight D. Eisenhower pledged America's "determination to help solve the fearful atomic dilemma—to devote its entire heart and mind to finding the way by which the miraculous inventiveness of man shall not be dedicated to his death, but consecrated to his life." John F. Kennedy, seeking to break the logjam on nuclear disarmament, said, "The world was not meant to be a prison in which man awaits his execution."[13]

Rajiv Gandhi, addressing the UN General Assembly on June 9, 1988, appealed, "Nuclear war will not mean the death of a hundred million people. Or even a thousand million. It will mean the extinction of four thousand million: the end of life as we know it on our planet Earth. We come to the United Nations to seek your support. We seek your support to put a stop to this madness."

Ronald Reagan called for the abolishment of "all nuclear weapons," which he considered to be "totally irrational, totally inhumane, good for nothing but killing, possibly destructive of life on earth and civilization." Mikhail Gorbachev shared this vision, which had also been expressed by previous American presidents.

Although Reagan and Mr. Gorbachev failed at Reykjavik to achieve the goal of an agreement to get rid of all nuclear weapons, they did succeed in turning the arms race on its head. They initiated steps leading to significant reductions in deployed long- and intermediate-range nuclear forces, including the elimination of an entire class of threatening missiles.

What will it take to rekindle the vision shared by Reagan and Mr. Gorbachev? Can a worldwide consensus be forged that defines a series of practical steps leading to major reductions in the nuclear danger? There is an urgent need to address the challenge posed by these two questions.

The Non-Proliferation Treaty (NPT) envisioned the end of all nuclear weapons. It provides (a) that states that did not possess nuclear weapons as of 1967 agree not to obtain them, and (b) that states that do possess them agree to divest themselves of these weapons over time. Every president of both parties since Richard Nixon has reaffirmed these treaty obligations, but nonnuclear weapon states have grown increasingly skeptical of the sincerity of the nuclear powers.

Strong nonproliferation efforts are under way. The Cooperative Threat Reduction program, the Global Threat Reduction Initiative, the Proliferation Security Initiative, and the Additional Protocols are innovative approaches that provide powerful new tools for detecting activities that violate the NPT and endanger world security. They deserve full implementation. The negotiations on proliferation of nuclear weapons by North Korea and Iran, involving all the permanent members of the Security Council plus Germany and Japan, are crucially important. They must be energetically pursued.

But by themselves, none of these steps are adequate to the danger. Reagan and General Secretary Gorbachev aspired to accomplish more at their meeting in Reykjavik twenty years ago: the elimination of nuclear weapons altogether. Their vision shocked experts in the doctrine of nuclear deterrence but galvanized the hopes of people around the world. The leaders of the two countries with the largest arsenals of nuclear weapons discussed the abolition of their most powerful weapons.

* * *

What should be done? Can the promise of the NPT and the possibilities envisioned at Reykjavik be brought to fruition? We believe that a major effort should be launched by the United States to produce a positive answer through concrete stages.

First and foremost is intensive work with leaders of the countries in possession of nuclear weapons to turn the goal of a world without nuclear weapons into a joint enterprise. Such a joint enterprise, by involving changes in the disposition of the states possessing nuclear weapons, would lend additional weight to efforts already under way to avoid the emergence of a nuclear-armed North Korea and Iran.

The program on which agreements should be sought would constitute a series of agreed and urgent steps that would lay the groundwork for a world free of the nuclear threat. Steps would include:

- Changing the Cold War posture of deployed nuclear weapons to increase warning time and thereby reduce the danger of an accidental or unauthorized use of a nuclear weapon.
- Continuing to reduce substantially the size of nuclear forces in all states that possess them.
- Eliminating short-range nuclear weapons designed to be forward-deployed.
- Initiating a bipartisan process with the Senate, including understandings to increase confidence and provide for periodic review, to achieve ratification of the Comprehensive Test Ban Treaty, taking advantage of recent technical advances, and working to secure ratification by other key states.
- Providing the highest possible standards of security for all stocks of weapons, weapons-usable plutonium, and highly enriched uranium everywhere in the world.
- Getting control of the uranium enrichment process, combined with the guarantee that uranium for nuclear power reactors could be obtained at a reasonable price,

first from the Nuclear Suppliers Group and then from the International Atomic Energy Agency (IAEA) or other controlled international reserves. It will also be necessary to deal with proliferation issues presented by spent fuel from reactors producing electricity.

- Halting the production of fissile material for weapons globally; phasing out the use of highly enriched uranium in civil commerce and removing weapons-usable uranium from research facilities around the world and rendering the materials safe.
- Redoubling our efforts to resolve regional confrontations and conflicts that give rise to new nuclear powers.

Achieving the goal of a world free of nuclear weapons will also require effective measures to impede or counter any nuclear-related conduct that is potentially threatening to the security of any state or peoples.

Reassertion of the vision of a world free of nuclear weapons and practical measures toward achieving that goal would be, and would be perceived as, a bold initiative consistent with America's moral heritage. The effort could have a profoundly positive impact on the security of future generations. Without the bold vision, the actions will not be perceived as fair or urgent. Without the actions, the vision will not be perceived as realistic or possible.

We endorse setting the goal of a world free of nuclear weapons and working energetically on the actions required to achieve that goal, beginning with the measures outlined above.

DETERRENCE IN THE AGE OF NUCLEAR PROLIFERATION

George P. Shultz, William J. Perry, Henry A. Kissinger, and Sam Nunn

Originally published in the Wall Street Journal *on March 7, 2011. Mr. Perry was secretary of defense from 1994 to 1997. Mr. Kissinger was secretary of state from 1973 to 1977. Mr. Nunn is the former chairman of the Senate Armed Services Committee.*

As long as there has been war, there have been efforts to deter actions a nation considers threatening. Until fairly recently, this meant building a military establishment capable of intimidating the adversary, defeating him, or making his victory more costly than the projected gains. This, with conventional weapons, took time. Deterrence and war strategy were identical.

The advent of the nuclear weapon introduced entirely new factors. It was possible, for the first time, to inflict at the beginning of a war the maximum casualties. The doctrine of mutual assured destruction represented this reality. Deterrence based on nuclear weapons, therefore, has three elements:

- It is importantly psychological, depending on calculations for which there is no historical experience. It is therefore precarious.
- It is devastating. An unrestrained nuclear exchange between superpowers could destroy civilized life as we know it in days.
- Mutual assured destruction raises enormous inhibitions against employing the weapons.

Since the first use of nuclear weapons against Japan, neither of the superpowers, nor any other country, has used nuclear weapons in a war. A gap opened between the psychological element of deterrence and the risks most leaders were willing to incur. US defense leaders made serious efforts to give the president more flexible options for nuclear use short of global annihilation. They never solved the problem, and it was always recognized that Washington and Moscow both held the keys to unpredictable and potentially catastrophic escalations.

As a result, nuclear deterrence was useful in preventing only the most catastrophic scenarios, which would have threatened our survival. But even with the deployment of thousands of nuclear weapons on both sides of the Iron Curtain, Soviet moves into Hungary in 1956 and Czechoslovakia in 1968 were not deterred. Nor were the numerous crises involving Berlin, including the building of the Wall in 1961, or major wars in Korea and Vietnam, or the Soviet invasion of Afghanistan in 1979. In the case of the Soviet Union, nuclear weapons did not prevent collapse or regime change.

Today, the Cold War is almost twenty years behind us, but many leaders and publics cannot conceive of deterrence without a strategy of mutual assured destruction. We have written previously that reliance on this strategy is becoming increasingly hazardous. With the spread of nuclear weapons, technology, materials, and know-how, there is an increasing risk that nuclear weapons will be used.

It is not possible to replicate the high-risk stability that prevailed between the two nuclear superpowers during the Cold War in such an environment. The growing number of nations with nuclear arms and differing motives, aims, and ambitions poses very high and unpredictable risks and increased instability.

From 1945 to 1991, America and the Soviet Union were diligent, professional, but also lucky that nuclear weapons were never used. Does the world want to continue to bet its survival on continued good fortune with a growing number of nuclear nations and adversaries globally? Can we devise and successfully implement with other nations, including other nuclear powers, careful, cooperative concepts to safely dismount the nuclear tiger while strengthening the capacity to assure our security and that of allies and other countries considered essential to our national security?

Recently, the four of us met at the Hoover Institution with a group of policy experts to discuss the possibilities for establishing a safer and more comprehensive form of deterrence and prevention in a world where the roles and risks of nuclear weapons are reduced and ultimately eliminated. Our broad conclusion is that nations should move forward together with a series of conceptual and practical steps toward deterrence that do not rely primarily on nuclear weapons or nuclear threats to maintain international peace and security.

The first step is to recognize that there is a daunting new spectrum of global security threats. These threats include chemical, biological, and radiological weapons, catastrophic terrorism and cyber warfare, as well as natural disasters resulting from climate change or other environmental problems, and health-related crises. For the United States and many other nations, existential threats relating to the very survival of the state have diminished, largely because of the end of the Cold War and the increasing realization that our common interests greatly exceed our differences. However, an accident or mistake involving nuclear weapons—or nuclear terrorism fueled by the spread of nuclear weapons, nuclear materials, and nuclear know-how—is still a very real risk. An effective strategy to deal with these dangers must be developed.

The second step is the realization that continued reliance on nuclear weapons as the principal element for deterrence is encouraging, or at least excusing, the spread of these weapons and will inevitably erode the essential cooperation necessary to avoid proliferation, protect nuclear materials, and deal effectively with new threats.

Third, the United States and Russia have no basis for maintaining a structure of deterrence involving nuclear weapons deployed in ways that increase the danger of an accidental or unauthorized use of a nuclear weapon, or even a deliberate nuclear exchange based on a false warning. Reducing the number of operationally deployed strategic nuclear warheads and delivery vehicles with verification to the levels set by the New START Treaty is an important step in reducing nuclear risks. Deeper nuclear reductions and changes in nuclear force posture involving the two nations should remain a priority. Further steps must include short-range tactical nuclear weapons.

Fourth, as long as nuclear weapons exist, America must retain a safe, secure, and reliable nuclear stockpile primarily to deter a nuclear attack and to reassure our allies through extended deterrence. There is an inherent limit to US and Russian nuclear reductions if other nuclear weapon states build up their inventories or if new nuclear powers emerge.

It is clear, however, that the United States and Russia—having led the nuclear buildup for decades—must continue to lead the build-down. The United States and its NATO allies, together with Russia, must begin moving away from threatening force postures and deployments, including the retention of thousands of short-range battlefield nuclear weapons. All conventional deployments should be reviewed from the aspect of provocation. This will make America, Russia, and Europe more secure. It will also set an example for the world.

Fifth, we recognize that for some nations, nuclear weapons may continue to appear relevant to their immediate security. There are certain undeniable dynamics in play—for example, the emergence of a nuclear-armed neighbor, or the perception of inferiority in conventional forces—that if not addressed could lead to the further proliferation of nuclear weapons and an increased risk they will be used. Thus, while the four of us believe that reliance on nuclear weapons for deterrence is becoming increasingly hazardous and decreasingly effective, some nations will hesitate to draw or act on the same conclusion unless regional confrontations and conflicts are addressed. We must therefore redouble our efforts to resolve these issues.

Achieving deterrence with assured security will require work by leaders and citizens on a range of issues, beginning with a clearer understanding of existing and emerging security threats. The role of nonnuclear means of deterrence to effectively prevent conflict and increase stability in troubled regions is a vital issue. Changes to extended deterrence must be developed over time by the United States and allies working closely together. Reconciling national perspectives on nuclear deterrence is a challenging problem, and comprehensive solutions must be developed. A world without nuclear weapons will not simply be today's world minus nuclear weapons.

Nations can, however, now begin moving together toward a safer and more stable form of deterrence. Progress must be made through a joint enterprise among nations, recognizing the need for greater cooperation, transparency, and verification to create the global political environment for stability and enhanced mutual security. Ensuring that nuclear materials are protected globally in order to limit any country's ability to reconstitute nuclear weapons and prevent terrorists from acquiring the material to build a crude nuclear bomb is a top priority.

Moving from mutual assured destruction toward a new and more stable form of deterrence with decreasing nuclear risks and an increasing measure of assured security for all nations could prevent our worst nightmare from becoming a reality, and it could have a profoundly positive impact on the security of future generations.

LENTEN NUKES

Right Reverend William E. Swing

A sermon by the Right Reverend William E. Swing based on the Gospel According to Mark, verses 8:31–38, Grace Cathedral, San Francisco, February 25, 2018.

The only, only good thing about the massive nuclear proliferation that is going on today is that it compels us to imagine the end of the world. That is spiritually healthy. That is the kind of imagination that Jesus had.

How much imagination does it take to picture the end of the world, now? India's first nuclear fleet became operational two years ago. China is expected to deploy a new road-mobile ICBM this year. Russia is modernizing its nuclear bombers and new nuclear submarines. Pakistan is aiming for nuclear ballistic and cruise capability. The UK is investing in new and improved nuclear ballistic missiles. The United States is refurbishing our nuclear weapons to the tune of $1.2 trillion dollars over the next decades. And the United States is calling for more small nuclear bombs, about the size used on Hiroshima and Nagasaki, so that we can surgically eliminate cities when needed. And . . . we are trying out the policy of "first use," dropping the bombs on others before they can drop them on us.

It doesn't take a prophet or a poet to point out that we are rushing toward the moment of self-destruction of life on this planet. All the while, we fantasize that our deliberations are only about national security and reality. This past summer, the United States ambassador to the United Nations said, "There is nothing I want more for my family than a world free of nuclear weapons. But . . . we have to be realistic." Ah, there it is. The ultimate choice. A fairy tale world free of nuclear weapons or a realistic world of nuclear weapons proliferating endlessly and among competing nations. In that contest, the prevailing wisdom today is that the more nuclear weapons we and our enemies have, the safer the world will be.

For 4.5 billion years, the world has been free of nuclear weapons, and we muddled along and evolved. But for the last seventy-three years, we have had nuclear weapons. And the world has not gone up in flames. Thus, brimming with confidence, this world's most armed political regimes and their politicians are betting that they can control nuclear weapons indefinitely and that no human errors or glitches in triggered systems will ever lead to an unmitigated apocalypse. And thus we dangle in their assurance to us.

This is where Jesus comes in. He says to his closest follower, "You are setting your mind *not* on divine things but on human things." It is easy to set your mind on human things. We happen to be human, and we tend to make decisions based on now, with only a fragile guess about our future. Divine thinking takes into consideration the end of the story. Hauntingly, Jesus says to us this morning, "What will it profit [you in the end], if [you] gain the whole world and forfeit your life?"

Translating those words into this moment of nuclear peril, we might say, "What does it profit the nation to have nuclear superiority over the rest of the nuclear nations if it sets up the scenario of a global thermonuclear war and the end of life on this planet?" "What will it profit you . . . ?" Or put another way, who wins the game of total extinction?

Here's is how I read the gospel lesson today. Jesus is saying, "You think you know how to handle ultimate power responsibly? Only God, who is the Beginning and the End, handles ultimate power responsibly." When you and I posture with endgame weapons, we are just playing God as we pretend to hold sway over this planet. Is that blasphemy? For Jesus, ultimate power on this planet is a revelation, not an explosion. Jesus has a pretty simple message: take the low road, follow me, live in a God-intoxicated world, suffer, die, and live a life of resurrection. The answer is in the back of the book. Live the answer.

In 2018, with nuclear proliferation, the options become stark. Either annihilation or resurrection. We are late in the game and time is running out. Today we are driving fast toward the cliff, and our leaders demand that we hit the accelerator, now. With gusto! That's the annihilation way to drive. The resurrection way to drive is to slow down, imagine the cliff that is just ahead, and begin to figure out how to stop this mad dash. Resurrection means learning to live on the other side of the death that beckons.

In the Jesus story, life after death was not referring to heaven. After his death, Jesus did not go to heaven. He came back to this earth. Earth! Here! This is where resurrection happens for Jesus, and He invites us into it. His fervent prayer was "On earth as it is in heaven." Or as the angel said in the book of Revelation, "Hurt not the earth." Jesus was focused on earth. Don't you dare blow it up!

Resurrection living means a vision of a righteous conclusion to this world's intractable opposites. Resurrection is the situation where Trump supporters and detractors figure out how to get along . . . where North and South Korea figure out how to be one . . . where Israel and the Palestinians discover room for everyone . . . where we learn to preserve the earth and make money at the same time . . . where people of one religion are taught to respect the people of other religions. Living into the ultimate solutions is resurrection living. You can't have it both ways: either annihilation or resurrection.

At the most recent State of the Union address, these words were spoken: "Perhaps someday in the future, there will be a magical moment when the countries of the world will get together to eliminate nuclear weapons." Today, I want to go on record and say that I believe in magic. That is part of what I mean when I recite the Creed and say, I believe in the Resurrection of the dead." Living, suffering, dying, and rising from the dead to create a new order of life is far more appealing to me than driving, full throttle, toward the nuclear annihilation of life on this earth.

Resurrection takes the long view and acknowledges that earth is the Lord's. Annihilation takes the short view and accepts that the politicians of the moment and the industrial-military complex of the moment have the right to destroy the earth. In our lesson this morning, Jesus says, "Get behind me, Satan! For you are setting your mind NOT on divine things but on human things."

At the biblical beginning of life, there was the choice of the apple or paradise. In the midst of life, there was the biblical choice of the empire or the cross. At the end of life, we have the same old choices, but now they are in the context of annihilation or resurrection.

And choices have consequences. Finally, at the end of time, the Author of life will return to this created and well-loved earth and demand accountability of us for what we did to enhance or destroy it. On that Day of Judgment, our precious bombs won't amount to a hill of beans. "What does it profit [you in the end] if [you] gain the whole world and forfeit your life?" Amen.

Acknowledgments

I had a great deal of help in assembling and organizing materials for this book. Judy Leep sifted through my collection in the Hoover Archives to locate speeches and testimony that I gave in earlier years and to provide me with the opportunity to select documents from the past that resonate today. David Fedor and James Cunningham assisted me in preparing the manuscript. David, in particular, helped me develop the introductions to each chapter, and David and Susan Southworth combed through my collection to find appropriate photographs. Tunku Varadarajan aided me with the introduction. I am deeply grateful to all of them for their essential assistance.

I was also the beneficiary of continual inspiration and support from my wife, Charlotte, to whom I dedicate this book.

Notes

1. Plenary session transcript, 14th Annual Meeting of the Valdai Discussion Club, Sochi, Russia, October 19, 2017.

2. United States Department of Defense, "Nuclear Posture Review," February 2018.

3. Margaret Thatcher, "Speech to Conservative Party Conference," Brighton, October 12, 1984.

4. George P. Shultz, "Terrorism and the Modern World," Park Avenue Synagogue, New York, October 25, 1984.

5. Heads of the Group of Seven, "Statement on International Terrorism, Tokyo Summit," Tokyo, May 5, 1986.

6. "The Story of the Sewing Machine: Its Invention, Improvements, and Social, Industrial and Commercial Importance," *New York Times*, January 7, 1860.

7. Gary Becker, "The Failure of the War on Drugs," March 20, 2005, Becker-Posner Blog, http://www.becker-posner-blog.com/2005 /03/the-failure-of-the-war-on-drugs-becker.html; "Response on Legalizing Drugs," March 27, 2005, Becker-Posner Blog, http://www.becker -posner-blog.com/2005/03/response-on-legalizing-drugs-becker.html; "The American War on Drugs Is Not Only an American Disaster," December 12, 2010, Becker-Posner Blog, http://www.becker-posner -blog.com/2010/12/the-american-war-on-drugs-is-not-only-an -american-disaster-becker.html; Glenn Greenwald, "Drug Decriminalization in Portugal: Lessons for Creating Fair and Successful Drug Policies," April 2, 2009, Cato Institute, https://www.cato.org/publications/ white-paper/drug-decriminalization-portugal-lessons-creating-fair -successful-drug-policies.

8. Nancy Reagan, "Address to the United Nations General Assembly Third Committee," New York, October 25, 1988.

9. Thomas Jefferson, "Letter to Jacob De La Motta" (September 9, 1820), in *Jews of the United States: 1790–1840*, ed. Joseph L. Blau and Salo W. Baron (New York: Columbia University Press, 1963).

10. Ronald Reagan, "Statement on Signing the Montreal Protocol on Ozone-Depleting Substances," April 5, 1988.

11. O. B. Toon, R. P. Turco, A. Robock, C. Bardeen, L. Oman, and G. L. Stenchikov, "Atmospheric Effects and Societal Consequences of Regional Scale Nuclear Conflicts and Acts of Individual Nuclear Terrorism," *Atmospheric Chemistry and Physics* (2007).

12. For more on these effects, see recent research by Lili Xia and Alan Robock, "Impacts of a Nuclear War in South Asia on Rice Production in Mainland China," *Climactic Change* 116, no. 2 (2013); A. Stenke, C. R. Hoyle, B. Luo, E. Rozanov, J. Gröbner, L. Maag, S. Brönnimann, and T. Peter, "Climate and Chemistry Effects of a Regional Scale Nuclear Conflict," *Atmospheric Chemistry and Physics* 13 (2013); and Michael Mills, Owen Toon, Julie Lee-Taylor, and Alan Robcock, "Multidecadal Global Cooling and Unprecedented Ozone Loss Following a Regional Nuclear Conflict," *Earth's Future* 2 (February 2014).

13. John F. Kennedy, "Annual Message to the Congress on the State of the Union." January 11, 1962.

About the Author

George Pratt Shultz is the Thomas W. and Susan B. Ford Distinguished Fellow at the Hoover Institution. He has had a distinguished career in government, in academia, and in the world of business. He is one of two individuals who have held four different federal cabinet posts; he has taught at three of this country's great universities; and for eight years he was president of a major engineering and construction company. Shultz was sworn in July 16, 1982, as the sixtieth US secretary of state under President Reagan, and served until January 20, 1989. He attended Princeton University, graduating with a BA in economics, whereupon he enlisted in the US Marine Corps, serving though 1945. He later earned a PhD in industrial economics from the Massachusetts Institute of Technology. In 1989, Shultz was awarded the Medal of Freedom, the nation's highest civilian honor. He is the author of many books, including *Issues on My Mind: Strategies for the Future* (2013) and *Learning from Experience* (2016), and served as editor of *Blueprint for America* (2016), and co-editor of *Beyond Disruption: Technology's Challenge to Governance* (2018).

Index